ON THE BUSES

THE COMPLETE STORY

ON THE BUSES

THE COMPLETE STORY

CRAIG WALKER

Forewords by Ronald Wolfe and Ronald Chesney

APEX PUBLISHING LTD

First published in hardback in 2009, updated and published in paperback by

Apex Publishing Ltd

12A St. John's Road, Clacton on Sea, Essex, CO15 4BP, United Kingdom

www.apexpublishing.co.uk

British Library Cataloguing-in-Publication Data
A catalogue record for this book
is available from the British Library

ISBN: 978-1-78281-851-9

Typeset in 11pt Baskerville Win95BT

Production Manager: Chris Cowlin

Cover Design: Hannah Blamires
Photograph: Kindly supplied by ITV

Printed and bound in the UK

CONTENTS

ACKNOWLEDGEMENTS

I would like to take this opportunity to thank the co-creators and co-writers of On The Buses, Ronald Wolfe and Ronald Chesney for theirpermission to write this book and then for writing such a marvellous foreword that truly compliments the book. Likewise, without clearance from Granada Media this book would not have been possible and I would also like to thank them for supplying the two images that appear on the book cover.

Filming locations required a lot of research and visits before confirmation. I would like to offer my thanks to film and television historian Rob Hickey whose invaluable local knowledge of Borehamwood enabled the finding of a number of previously unknown filming locations seen in the films. Thanks also goes out to members of my forum at www.onthebusesforum.org who were a great help unearthing new filming locations from the television series.

I would also like to acknowledge the invaluable following websites of www.imdb.com, www.ftvdb.bfi.org.uk, www.wikipedia.org and www.comedy.org.uk as each were a valuable source of information. I would also like to pay homage and thanks to Steve's pioneering website The Official On The Buses Fan Club at www.onthebusesfanclub.com which was not only a great help but Steve has also offered great support to the project. Another great source of information was the tribute site at www.t0ester.co.uk/otb/otbindex which is a must see site for all On The Buses fans. Big thanks to experienced author Kevin Snelgrove for his very helpful advice and encouragement in what is my first attempt at writing a book. Also a big help throughout this exciting project was my sister Michelle so a big special thanks for all the support and help in acting as an agent.

Thanks must also go to Linda Regan, Ursula Mohan and Hal Dyer for their kind words about this book. Last and certainly not least the man to thank for this book making it into print is Chris Cowlin and all at Apex Publishing Ltd for taking this project on and having faith in the book you are about to read.

FOREWORD

It is very gratifying to be asked to write the foreword to a book on a subject we know very well – the TV sitcom series On The Buses – and which contains a mine of information, some of which we were not familiar with and are now very grateful to learn about. The details that Craig Walker has unearthed are both fascinating and staggering: a cornucopia of facts covering every episode and every aspect of the series and, well, just about everything a fan would ever want to know, including the making of the three On The Buses feature films that followed.

As we write, On The Buses has just celebrated its 40th birthday, and it is still as hale and hearty as ever. But let us go back to 1969, the year it was born. Having earlier written two successful TV series, The Rag Trade and Meet the Wife, it was time, we hoped, for another hit show. We had been working for some time on an idea about a bus driver and his life both at work and at home. Only just a short time before, London Weekend Television had started operating, and, although they opened in a blaze of glory and high hopes, their first year was pretty much a disaster. So now they were desperately looking for some new shows, For us, it couldn't have been better timing or a more promising opportunity.

At this time, Frank Muir was Head of London Weekend Television's Light Entertainment Department. We knew Frank from way back, when, with his then writing partner, Denis Norden, he wrote extremely successful radio and TV sitcoms. We got in touch with him, made an appointment, and headed for LWT. We remember it well. It was five o'clock on a Friday afternoon. We handed him the format, which he skimmed through with his practised eye. Did we see the semblance of a smile? He then dashed off to have a quick word with Cyril Bennett, the Programme Controller. At roughly twenty-past-five we were offered a contract – pretty surprising really, as only the previous week this same format had been rejected by the BBC.

The title we had decided on was 'On The Buses', which we felt said everything. We had given the show a great deal of thought over a prolonged period of time, and we knew that if most of the cast were featured in uniform they would be immediately identifiable. There would be two different set-ups: life at the bus garage and in the home. We figured that these two situations would give a platform for the many conflicts arising in both camps.

So, with the idea approved by London Weekend Television, we wrote the first script and several storylines. Things went well up to that point, but we then had to go through the agonising game of chance called 'casting'.

We knew, both by instinct and by his past performances, that Reg Varney would be perfect as the bus driver. By a stroke of luck, Stuart Allen, Producer/Director of most of the series and really great at casting, led us to Stephen Lewis, who was chosen as the Inspector. He had been working in a production at Stratford East called Mrs Wilson's Diary, and in that same show was Bob Grant, who was invited to play the part of Jack, the Conductor.

We did not have to look too far for an ideal actress to fill the role of Stan's mum – the first and immediate choice was Doris Hare. Alas, she was out of the country with her husband, a Professor of Medicine, who was attending a seminar. So Cicely Courtneidge was booked for the first series on the understanding that, if the show was successful and continued, she would be replaced by Doris. And that is how it turned out.

The part of Olive was much more difficult. There are not many actresses who would have been willing to take on the role of Stan's sister - a plain, dumpy, somewhat thick and most unattractive lady. And then we thought of Anna Karen, whom we had cast in an earlier sitcom in which she had played a similarly unattractive role, and which she had done magnificently. And it certainly wasn't typecasting; in reality she is a most attractive lady, and it needed a great deal of work on the part of the make-up department before she began to look as she appeared in the show. Michael Robbins, who played the part of Olive's husband, Arthur, was just perfect for the part too.

So we had our main cast, and it was now up to the viewers, once the show was transmitted, to declare it a hit or a miss!

Well, the show was reckoned by a lot of people to be crude and vulgar – very working-class. But this was the kind of show we wrote and we seemed to be quite good at it. Very predictably, it was panned by the critics and the reviews were pretty awful ... but the viewing figures were huge – numbers grew to 16 million and On The Buses very soon climbed to the top of the ratings. As far as the public were concerned, it was a series not to be missed.

Before long, the actors became overnight celebrities. They were recognised and mobbed by autograph hunters, and when the show was at its height Bob Grant got married at Caxton Hall. Of course, the whole cast attended and the police had to control the crowd, which was estimated to run into several thousand.

So our TV sitcom, which started life 40 years ago without any fanfare or much publicity, became an unexpectedly huge hit, and with the advent of DVDs and occasional repeats, it looks as though it still has some mileage left.

If you are already a fan, read the book and enjoy. If you are not a fan, read the book, enjoy, and become one. For us, it has been an incredible journey of nostalgia – which, to quote the logo of the On The Buses Fan Club, never goes out of fashion!

Best wishes
Ronald Chesney and Ronald Wolfe
Creators of 'On The Buses'

INTRODUCTION

During the 1960s and 1970s British television was awash with classic sitcoms, but one of those almost didn't make it onto the screens. The successful comedy-writing team of Ronald Wolfe and Ronald Chesney had written a new sitcom about a couple of busmen and took the idea to the BBC, but they were not impressed and rejected it. With a strong belief in their plot and its potential, Wolfe and Chesney were not to be put off and approached newly formed London Weekend Television and they accepted the idea.

Further problems lay ahead though, as LWT weren't fully convinced with the casting. Ronald Wolfe and Ronald Chesney had written the main role of bus driver Stan Butler with actor and entertainer Reg Varney in mind. Reg had worked on their hit sitcom The Rag Trade with great success and they knew he was the right man for the part. LWT were supposedly keen on another actor for the role and in some quarters Ronnie Barker had been linked with the part, but Wolfe and Chesney had their way in the end and Reg Varney's performances as Stan Butler were to leave no one with any regrets.

Another problem to overcome before the sitcom could go into production was that Ronald Wolfe and Ronald Chesney needed the use of a bus depot and a fleet of buses. London Transport were approached but felt that the sitcom would be bad for their public image, portraying their buses as unpunctual and staff as lazy and ill-disciplined, and so refused to allow their buses to be used. Undaunted, Ronald Wolfe and Ronald Chesney went to the Eastern National bus company and thankfully for us all they were happy for their buses to be used. And so On The Buses was finally given the green light.

It was on Friday 28th February 1969 at 7.30 p.m. that we first heard the ringing of a bus bell and Bob Grant saying: “Hold very tightly please,” followed by the rolling of the opening credits accompanied by the now famous ‘Happy Larry’ theme music, which was composed by Tony Russell. After overcoming various stumbling blocks, On The Buses was finally on air and it soon proved to be a massive hit with the British viewing public. The humour was non-politically correct and laden with innuendo, double entendres and slick one-liners that were so popular in British sitcoms of that era. The scripts were and still are of the highest order and the cast consisting of Reg Varney, Bob Grant, Stephen Lewis, Anna Karen, Michael Robbins, Cicely Courtneidge and Doris Hare had a great chemistry and superb comedic timing. With this rich blend of comedy talent backed by Wolfe and Chesney scripts, On The Buses was destined to become, in my opinion, the greatest sitcom of all-time.

On The Buses was to run for a total of seven series from 1969 to 1973 with a total of seventy-four episodes, spawning three spin-off films with varying success at the box office. There was also an American version called Lotsa Luck in 1973, and a year after the end of On The Buses a spin-off sitcom called Don’t Drink The Water aired in 1974.The story didn’t quite end there, as in 1991 there was a set of scripts in place for a new sitcom to be called Back On The Buses, which was to have seen all the original cast reunited, with the plot following a retired Stan Butler running his own coach company. With a pilot episode set to be filmed the project fell through at the latter stages.

Even though critics today pan it as crude and sexist, On The Buses never resorted to any swearing or sex scenes to gain laughs and thrills and it still remains hugely popular today, earning a new generation of fans. Its popularity is not just confined to Britain, however, as it has big fan bases in all corners of the world ranging from as far afield as Canada and Australia. On The Buses is a comedy phenomenon that refuses to die and that trait is only held by legends of comedy such as Laurel and Hardy, Charlie Chaplin, 'Carry On' films and such a legend deserves a book to pay homage to it, which is my motivation for the book you are about to read.

ABOUT THE CAST

REG VARNEY (Reginald Alfred Varney)

Date of Birth: 11th July 1916
Birthplace: Canning Town, London
Died: 16th November 2008
On The Buses Debut: Series 1, Episode 1 – 'The Early Shift'
On The Buses Episode Appearances: 68
On The Buses Film Appearances: 3

Career

Reg Varney's launch into show business stemmed from his taking piano lessons as a child. He grew to become a highly talented pianist and appeared in working men's clubs, public houses and cinemas in the East End of London. In his twenties Reg worked non-stop playing in clubs and singing with big bands.

It was the onset of the Second World War that began to shape Reg Varney's career as club work dried up. Reg enlisted with the Royal Engineers and he performed regularly for the troops and toured the Far East. His style of playing the piano with such energy mixed with his small stature raised many laughs as his feet struggled to reach the pedals. The laughs gained, though unintentional, encouraged Reg to integrate more comedy into his act, and so a new comedy star was born.

After the end of the Second World War Reg demobbed and

became an all-round entertainer working in music halls. He appeared on stage in the late 1940s in a comic revue called Gaytime and his straight man was a young entertainer called Benny Hill. Their highly successful act progressed onto television in 1947 and Reg Varney's career really began to take off.

It was in 1961 that Reg first worked with writers Ronald Wolfe and Ronald Chesney on the BBC sitcom The Rag Trade. It was a big hit, which ran for two years with three series and thirty-six episodes. This hit sitcom made Reg Varney highly sought after and he went on to star in other hit sitcoms such as Beggar My Neighbour as well as appearing in variety shows. It was in 1969 that Reg starred in the new Wolfe and Chesney sitcom On The Buses and this really made him a household name.

On The Buses was a huge hit, spawning three spin-off films and running from 1969 to 1973 over seven TV series, but Reg bowed out midway through the last series. This left him open to doing a series of cabaret shows, something that Reg always loved.

Reg's career began to wind down in the mid-1970s, but he did appear in one more sitcom called Down the 'Gate, although this never reached the heights achieved by On The Buses or The Rag Trade. Reg Varney had one last hit to his name when he appeared in the remake of the silent film The Plank.

For a number of years Reg's career continued on stage. He went on tour of Australia, Canada and New Zealand with his cabaret act and was also involved in a stage version of On The Buses in 1988.

It was during the 1990s, as he neared the age of 80, that Reg Varney was forced to retire due to ill health. He lived in both Devon and Malta during his retirement and enjoyed painting. Sadly, on 16th November 2008, after a short illness due to a chest infection, Reg Varney passed away in a nursing home in Budleigh Salterton in Devon at the age of 92.

Reg will be best remembered for his role as Stan Butler, but he was a truly talented all-round entertainer who had worked with some of the best comedy actors of all time, including Benny Hill, Sid James, James Robertson Justice, Margaret Rutherford, Barbara Windsor, Esma Cannon, Irene Handl, Frankie Howerd, Eric Barker, Terry Scott, June Whitfield, Ted Ray, Pat Coombs and all of the On The Buses cast. He will be sadly missed as a great comedy actor and a gentleman who always had time for his fans.

Filmography

Film

Miss Robin Hood (1952)
Joey Boy (1965)
The Great St Trinian's Train Robbery (1966)
On The Buses (1971)
The Best Pair of Legs in the Business (1972)
Mutiny On The Buses (1972)
Go For A Take (1972)
Holiday On The Buses (1973)

Television

The Rag Trade (1961-1963)
The Valiant Varney's (1964-1965)
Beggar My Neighbour (1966-1968)
Hooray for Laughter (1967)
The Best Pair of Legs in the Business (1968)
The Rovers (1969)

On The Buses (1969-1973)
The Other Reg Varney (1970)
The Reg Varney Revue (1972)
Reg Varney (1973-1974)
Down the 'Gate (1975-1976)
The Plank (1979)
Red Peppers (1991)
Paul Merton's Life of Comedy (1995)

BOB GRANT (Robert St Clair Grant)

Date of Birth: 14th April 1932
Birthplace: Hammersmith, London
Died: 8th November 2003
On The Buses Debut: Series 1, Episode 1 – 'The Early Shift'
On The Buses Episode Appearances: 74
On The Buses Film Appearances: 3

Career

At an early age Bob Grant trained as an actor at the famous Royal Academy of Dramatic Arts (RADA) amidst jobs as a frozen food salesman and also as a bus conductor. He did his National Service with the Royal Artillery, achieving the rank of Lieutenant.

It was in repertory work that Bob had his first taste of show business, debuting in 1952 in a play called A Worm's Eye View. His stage career began to offer larger roles in bigger theatres and it was then that he moved on to television and big screen appearances. As was the case on stage, Bob began with small bit-part roles in various big productions, but then in 1969 his career really took off.

A starring role at the beginning of 1969 in the one-off comedy Mrs Wilson's Diary was quickly followed up by the part for which Bob Grant will always be best remembered - bus conductor Jack Harper in On The Buses. His toothy grin and his eye for the ladies made him a huge favourite of the fans. Bob was ever-present, appearing in all seventy-four episodes as well as the three spin-off films, and he also wrote a number of episodes of On The Buses along with co-star Stephen Lewis.

Amidst his massive success in On The Buses, Bob Grant was still actively involved in stage work and writing comedies with Stephen Lewis. One of their works, The Jugg Brothers, was aired on the famous BBC Comedy Playhouse series, but it never progressed into the anticipated full-blown sitcom.

When On The Buses came to an end in 1973 Bob Grant toured Australia, appearing in a stage version of No Sex, Please - We're British, and continued writing comedy for stage shows. In 1975 Bob starred alongside Anna Karen in another comedy he had written called Milk-O, about a milkman, which was aired in the UK but unfortunately progressed no further than the pilot episode.

Acting opportunities for Bob Grant gradually began to dry up apart from some stage work, although this was also becoming increasingly hard to come by. This lack of work and income led to his suffering from long bouts of depression. In the 1980s Bob's work was restricted almost entirely to pantomime appearances and circumstances weren't going to improve.

Tragically in 2003, after two previous failed attempts, Bob Grant committed suicide after suffering from manic depression for a number of years. It was a sad end to such a talented actor, who was woefully underused but is still remembered with great fondness to this day.

Filmography

Film

Sparrows Can't Sing (1963)
Till Death Us Do Part (1969)
On The Buses (1971)
Mutiny On The Buses (1972)
Holiday On The Buses (1973)

Television

Quatermass and the Pit (1959)
Sir Francis Drake (1962)
No Hiding Place (1963)
Softly, Softly (1967)
Z Cars (1968)
Mrs Wilson's Diary (1969)
On The Buses (1969-1973)
The Jugg Brothers (1970)
The Borderers (1970)
Milk-O (1975)

STEPHEN LEWIS (born Stephen Cato)

Date of Birth: 14th November 1936
Birthplace: London
On The Buses Debut: Series 1, Episode 1 – 'The Early Shift'
On The Buses Episode Appearances: 74
On The Buses Film Appearances: 3

Career

Stephen Lewis began his working life as a merchant seaman,

but following an audition with the well-known Theatre Workshop run by famed playwright and dramatist Joan Littlewood he moved into the show business trade in 1958. Stage work quickly followed and Stephen also displayed a talent for writing.

Stephen's first appearance on British television came in 1961 in the ITV Play of the Week series. A string of small roles on the big screen ensued, including Sparrows Can't Sing, which he had written. His first large role came in 1969 in the one-off comedy Mrs Wilson's Diary, starring alongside Bob Grant.

Later that year came Stephen Lewis's big breakthrough, when he was cast as the strict and morose bus inspector Cyril 'Blakey' Blake in the new sitcom On The Buses. His character became massive and his new catchphrase of "I 'ate you, Butler" was to become a must for all impressionists of the time and is still fondly remembered today. Stephen portrayed Inspector Blake in all seventy-four episodes and in the three spin-off films as well as co-writing a few episodes with Bob Grant.

Lewis also wrote and appeared in The Jugg Brothers with Bob Grant as part of the Comedy Playhouse series. Television roles in hit shows such as Manhunt and Father, Dear Father all came in 1970. As for the big screen, he had small roles in a couple of films, mostly notably rubbing shoulders with a star-studded cast in The Magnificent Seven Deadly Sins.

When On The Buses ended in 1973, a spin-off series penned by the Wolfe and Chesney partnership called Don't Drink the Water saw Stephen Lewis reprise his role as now retired Inspector Cyril Blake, who had moved to Spain with his sister (played by Pat Coombs). The sitcom never really took off, however, and the plug was pulled in 1975 after only two series.

A number of small roles in film and television as well as stage work kept Stephen active in show business until he became established as a regular on the everlasting sitcom Last of the Summer Wine in 1991. He played the character Smiler and remained in the cast for sixteen years. He remained active on stage during that time and was still sought after for other television productions. His next starring role was as Hatley railway station signalman Harry Lambert in the BBC sitcom Oh, Doctor Beeching! in 1995, which ran for a couple of series and a total of twenty episodes. Stephen Lewis's great career has seen him plying his trade in show business for half a century.

Filmography

Film

A Prize of Arms (1962)
Sparrows Can't Sing (1963)
Kaleidoscope (1966)
Negatives (1968)
Staircase (1969)
Some Will, Some Won't (1970)
On The Buses (1971)
The Magnificent Seven Deadly Sins (1971)
Mutiny On The Buses (1972)
Holiday On The Buses (1973)
Adventures of a Taxi Driver (1976)
The Last Remake of Beau Geste (1977)
Adventures of a Plumber's Mate (1978)
The McGuffin (1986)
Out of Order (1987)
Personal Services (1987)

The Krays (1990)

Television

ITV Play of the Week (1961)

Mrs Wilson's Diary (1969)

On The Buses (1969-1973)

The Jugg Brothers (1970)

Manhunt (1970)

Father, Dear Father (1970)

Don't Drink the Water (1974-1975)

The Fosters (1977)

Rep (1982)

Bodger and Badger (1989)

One Foot in the Grave (1991)

2 Point 4 Children (1991)

Look at It This Way (1992)

Last of the Summer Wine (1993-2006)

The Great Kandinsky (1995)

The All New Alexei Sayle Show (1995)

Oh, Doctor Beeching! (1995-1997)

Revolver (2001)

ANNA KAREN

Date of Birth: 19th September 1936

Birthplace: Durban, South Africa

On The Buses Debut: Series 1, Episode 1 – 'The Early Shift'

On The Buses Episode Appearances: 74

On The Buses Film Appearances: 3

Career

Prior to her acting career, Anna Karen worked as an exotic

dancer at London's Panama Club. However, she did have three years' training with the South African National Theatre before arriving in the United Kingdom in the early 1950s.

Anna's first dip into show business came with an appearance in a short docu-film called Nudist Memories in 1961. Stage work was on the agenda as well, but she had to wait five years for her next role in film or television, as an extra in the star-studded cast of a film called The Sandwich Man.

It was at the beginning of 1969 (a memorable year for Anna) that she made her British television debut in an episode of the Ronald Wolfe and Ronald Chesney sitcom Wild, Wild Women. Only a few weeks later, she was to become a household name as Olive, the bespectacled and neglected wife of Arthur in the hit sitcom On The Buses. It was a credit to the make-up crew on the show that Olive appeared so dowdy - quite a feat considering that Anna was formerly an attractive model and exotic dancer. Olive's inability to cook and her constant reminders to Arthur about his operation gained many laughs and made her a vital part of On The Buses. Anna remained in On The Buses for the entire seventy-four episodes and all three spin-off films.

Also in 1969, Anna Karen had the distinction of having a small role in the classic film Carry On Camping, in which she played the part of a teenager in school uniform even though in reality she was a 32-year-old woman. This was followed by another small role in Carry On Loving in 1970.

Television roles, although small, were plentiful for Anna until the latter half of the 1970s. Ronald Wolfe and Ronald Chesney wrote an updated version of their early 1960s hit sitcom The Rag Trade and Anna earned a starring role, reprising her On The Buses character, Olive. It was a fair success and ran for two series comprising twenty-two episodes from

1977 to 1978.

Active on stage and in pantomime throughout most of her career, Anna's next television role came in 1985 when she appeared in three episodes of what was, if truth be told, a very poor sitcom called Troubles and Strife. She also dipped her toes into the children's television shows Roland Rat (1986) and Super Gran (1987) and in 1996 had a fair-sized role in the comedy film Beautiful Thing.

In recent years Anna Karen has made a number of sporadic appearances in the hit British soap EastEnders, playing the part of Aunt Sal, the screen sister of Peggy Mitchell (played by Barbara Windsor - a long-time friend of Anna's). Anna is still active in show business to this day, almost 50 years after her acting career began.

Filmography

Film

Nudist Memories (1961)

The Sandwich Man (1966)

Poor Cow (1967)

Carry On Camping (1969)

Carry On Loving (1970)

On The Buses (1971)

Mutiny On The Buses (1972)

Holiday On The Buses (1973)

What's Up Nurse! (1977)

Beautiful Thing (1996)

Television

Wild, Wild Women (1969)

On The Buses (1969-1973)

Dixon of Dock Green (1970)

Milk-O (1975)

The Kenneth Williams Show (1976)
The Rag Trade (1977-1978)
Troubles and Strife (1985-1986)
Roland Rat: The Series (1986)
Super Gran (1987)
Goodnight Sweetheart (1998)
Boyz Unlimited (1999)
Revolver (2001)
EastEnders (2001-2008)
The Bill (2002)
The Second Quest (2004)
The Golden Hour (2005)

MICHAEL (Anthony) ROBBINS

Date of Birth: 14th November 1930
Birthplace: London
Died: 11th December 1992
On The Buses Debut: Series 1, Episode 1 – 'The Early Shift'
On The Buses Episode Appearances: 61
On The Buses Film Appearances: 3

Career

Michael Robbins was formerly a bank clerk and learnt the acting trade through a number of amateur dramatic performances before progressing on to ample work for various repertory companies. In repertory Michael worked alongside some of the best actors and actresses in the business such as Albert Finney, Bernard Braden, Barbara Windsor and Barbara Kelly, to name but a few.

The start of a packed television and film career began at the end of 1957 with an appearance in the sitcom Be Soon. Michael was very adept and versatile and drama appearances on TV soon followed, including his first film role in Lunch Hour in 1961. Proof of Michael's all-round talents came when he appeared in the 1963 musical film What a Crazy World. At the same time small roles in hit TV series such as Ghost Squad, The Avengers, The Baron, Gideon's Way, The Saint, Dixon of Dock Green, Z Cars and The Edgar Wallace Mystery Theatre flowed, together with small but plentiful film roles.

The biggest role of Michael's entire career came in 1969 when he was cast as the snobbish know-it-all Arthur Rudge (brother-in-law of Stan Butler) in On The Buses. His character always thwarted Stan's chances of romance with the clippies and was always quick to make snide remarks about his wife, Olive, as well as anxiously dodging her amorous advances. Arthur and Olive's far from domestic and marital bliss was an integral part of On The Buses, and Michael Robbins' dry wit was a joy to behold as he delivered his hilarious one-liners. Michael appeared in the first six series of On The Buses, from 1969 to 1972, as well as all three spin-off films, but opted out of the seventh series in order to return to stage work.

During his time performing in On The Buses Michael Robbins also appeared in notable films such as Till Death Us Do Part, Zeppelin and That's Your Funeral, and he took on further roles post-On The Buses in films of varying success such as No Sex Please: We're British (1973), Man about the House (1974), The Pink Panther Strikes Again (1976) and The Great Muppet Caper (1981).

Although starring roles were criminally rare after On The Buses, Michael regularly appeared in smash hit television series of all genres such as The Sweeney, The Good Life, Return of the Saint, George and Mildred, Dick Turpin and Minder, as well as a large role in a series of the cult BBC sci-fi programme Doctor Who in 1982. Also in the 1980s he continued his stage and pantomime career and he appeared alongside Anna Karen and Doris Hare in Canada in a play called On The Buses: A New Life, reprising his role of Arthur Rudge. Television roles continued apace in more hit series such as The Chinese Detective, The Bounder, Fresh Fields, Fairly Secret Army, Rumpole of the Bailey, Hi-de-Hi! and EastEnders.

Sadly, Michael Robbins was struck down by cancer and his last television work saw him appear in You Rang, M'Lord?, The Bill and finally the hit sitcom One Foot in the Grave. It was a great loss to us all when Michael lost his battle against cancer and passed away on 11th December 1992 at the age of 62.

Filmography

Film

Lunch Hour (1961)
A Prize of Arms (1962)
What a Crazy World (1963)
The Bargee (1964)
Rattle of a Simple Man (1964)
The Whisperers (1967)
Up the Junction (1968)
Till Death Us Do Part (1969)
The Looking Glass War (1969)
Crossplot (1969)
All the Way Up (1970)
Zeppelin (1971)

Villain (1971)
On The Buses (1971)
That's Your Funeral (1972)
Mutiny On The Buses (1972)
No Sex Please: We're British (1973)
Holiday On The Buses (1973)
Man about the House (1974)
The Pink Panther Strikes Again (1976)
The Great Muppet Caper (1981)
Victor Victoria (1972)
Just Ask for a Diamond (1988)

Television
Be Soon (1957)
BBC Sunday Night Theatre (1959)
On Trial (1960)
The Avengers (1961-1969)
You Can't Win (1961)
Armchair Theatre (1961-1968)
Studio Four (1962)
ITV Play of the Week (1962-1966)
Dimensions of Fear (1963)
Crane (1963)
The Plane Makers (1963)
Ghost Squad (1963-1964)
Z Cars (1963-1974)
Suspense (1963)
No Hiding Place (1964-1965)
The Four Seasons of Rosie Carr (1964)
Dixon of Dock Green (1964-1967)
Diary of a Young Man (1964)
Count of Monte Cristo (1964)

The Saint (1964-1968)
Gideon's Way (1965)
Sherlock Holmes (1965-1968)
Zero One (1965)
The Wednesday Thriller (1965)
Redcap (1965)
The Edgar Wallace Mystery Theatre (1965)
The Baron (1966)
The Man in Room 17 (1966)
Adam Adamant Lives (1966)
Thirteen Against Fate (1966)
Callan (1967)
Theatre 625 (1967)
The Pilgrim's Progress (1967)
The Gamblers (1967)
Les Misérables (1967)
State of the Union (1968)
ITV Playhouse (1968)
The First Lady (1968)
Hello, Good Evening and Welcome (1968)
On The Buses (1969-1972)
ITV Saturday Night Theatre (1969)
Department S (1969)
Judge Dee (1969)
Thirty-Minute Theatre (1969)
Play of the Month (1970)
Danton (1970)
Cider with Rosie (1971)
Comedy Playhouse (1973)
Soap Opera in Stockwell (1973)
Thick as Thieves (1974)
The Main Chance (1975)

Moody and Pegg (1975)
The Sweeney (1975)
Centre Play (1975)
Operation Patch (1976)
The Good Life (1976)
The Heavy Mob (1977)
Murder Most English: A Flaxborough Chronicle (1977)
The Fuzz (1977)
Devenish (1977-1978)
Mixed Blessings (1978)
Return of the Saint (1979)
Leave It to Charlie (1979)
George and Mildred (1979)
Play for Today (1980)
Dick Turpin (1980)
Minder (1980)
Brendon Chase (1981)
Emery Presents: Legacy of Murder (1982)
Doctor Who (1982)
The Chinese Detective (1982)
The Merry Wives of Windsor (1982)
PS, It's Paul Squire (1983)
The Bounder (1983)
Fairly Secret Army (1984)
Fresh Fields (1985)
Lost in London (1985)
Dempsey & Makepeace (1986)
Rumpole of the Bailey (1987)
Strong Poison (1987)
Hi-de-Hi! (1988)
EastEnders (1989)
The Bill (1989-1991)

One Foot in the Grave (1990-1991)
You Rang, M'Lord? (1990)
Adam Bede (1991)
The New Statesman (1991)

DORIS HARE

Date of Birth: 1st March 1905
Birthplace: Bargoed, Monmouthshire, Wales
Died: 30th May 2000
On The Buses Debut: Series 2 Episode 1 - Family Flu
On The Buses Episode Appearances: 67
On The Buses Film Appearances: 3

Career

Doris Hare was born into a family with acting in its blood, with her parents, brothers and sisters all in show business. Doris made her professional debut at the age three and went on to become a regular in music halls. She made her West End debut in The Scarlet Clue in 1916 and her stage work continued unabated for the rest of her life.

Stage and radio work became a staple diet for Doris after leaving school and kept her busy. Her career expanded to films in 1934 when she starred in a thriller called Night Mail and more film roles followed up until 1940. As the Second World War raged, Doris became a forces sweetheart and in 1941 she was awarded an MBE.

Following the war Doris's film career continued and in 1953 she made her television debut in the US series Douglas Fairbanks Jr, Presents. This was the first of many television appearances, which included The Avengers, The Benny Hill Show, The Saint, Dixon of Dock Green, The Ronnie Barker

Playhouse, Coronation Street, Randall and Hopkirk (Deceased), The Secret Diary of Adrian Mole, Aged 13¾ and Never the Twain.

Doris was unavailable for the start of On The Buses due to other work commitments, but at the start of the second series she took on the role of Stan and Olive's mother, Mabel Butler. Mabel was a very defensive woman who fiercely protected her offspring in the face of put-downs or mistreatment but also jealously took a dislike to any girlfriends Stan brought home and always found a way to wreck any hope he had of starting a relationship. Doris, with vast acting experience, made the part her own and continued in the role of Mrs Butler for all the remaining sixty-seven episodes and the three spin-off films over the next four years.

After the cameras had stopped rolling in On The Buses Doris proceeded with her stage work and in the mid-1970s had a starring role in three 'Confessions' films to further cement her name with the British public. Television roles continued to come her way and, even at the grand old age of 82, Doris had a starring role in the ITV sitcom The Growing Pains of Adrian Mole in 1987 and also in the hit British comedy film Nuns on the Run three years later. In 1992 Doris Hare's stage career finally came to an end at the London Palladium in an emotional tribute night to actress Evelyn Laye.

Doris Hare sadly passed away at the age of 95 at Denville Hall (a retirement home for actors) in Northwood, Middlesex. A long, wonderful life in show business had come to an end, but Doris will always be remembered for all her acting work over such an incredible length of time.

Filmography

Film

Night Mail (1934)
Opening Night (1935)
Jubilee Window (1935)
Luck of the Navy (1938)
Discoveries (1939)
She Couldn't Say No (1940)
Here Come The Huggetts (1948)
The History of Mr Polly (1949)
Dance Hall (1950)
Thought to Kill (1954)
Double Exposure (1954)
Tiger by the Tail (1955)
No Smoking (1955)
Strangers Meeting (1957)
Another Time, Another Place (1958)
The League of Gentlemen (1960)
A Place to Go (1963)
Day of Rest (1970)
On The Buses (1971)
Mutiny On The Buses (1972)
Holiday On The Buses (1973)
Confessions of a Pop Performer (1975)
Confessions of a Driving Instructor (1976)
Confessions from a Holiday Camp (1977)
Nuns on the Run (1990)
Second Best (1994)

Television

Douglas Fairbanks Jr, Presents (1953-1956)
Colonel March of Scotland Yard (1956)

Dixon of Dock Green (1961-1966)
Alfred Marks Time (1961)
The Avengers (1961)
No Hiding Place (1961)
Comedy Playhouse (1963)
Armchair Mystery Theatre (1964)
Esther Waters (1964)
The Benny Hill Show (1965)
The Saint (1965)
Thirty-Minute Theatre (1968)
The Ronnie Barker Playhouse (1968)
Theatre 625 (1968)
Coronation Street (1968-1969)
Mr Digby Darling (1969)
On The Buses (1969-1973)
Randall and Hopkirk (Deceased) (1969)
Three Piece Suite (1977)
BBC2 Play of the Week (1977)
Why Didn't They Ask Evans? (1980)
Diamonds (1981)
Nanny (1982)
The Secret Diary of Adrian Mole, Aged 13¾ (1985)
Comrade Dad (1986)
Never the Twain (1986)
The Growing Pains of Adrian Mole (1987)
Stuff (1988)

CICELY COURTNEIDGE

Date of Birth: 1st April 1893
Birthplace: Sydney, Australia
Died: 26th April 1980
On The Buses Debut: Series 1 Episode 1 - The Early Shift
On The Buses Episode Appearances: 7
On The Buses Film Appearances: 0

Career

Cicely Courtneidge's show business career began in theatre and the actress was to become a household name, with a string of film appearances in the 1930s. The comedy thriller The Ghost Train (1931) started the ball rolling and in the majority of her work during that decade she appeared alongside her husband, Jack Hulbert. Cicely excelled in film and stage work but she also branched out into television work.

In 1961 on US television Cicely appeared in an episode of Kraft Mystery Theatre and her British television debut came in the crime series Man of the World in 1963. Two years later, on the big screen, Cicely had a small role in the star-studded smash hit film Those Magnificent Men in Their Flying Machines and followed this up with a part in the comedy film The Wrong Box.

In 1969, Cicely was cast for the part of Mrs Butler in On The Buses, as the first choice Doris Hare was unavailable for the first series. Cicely's character portrayal was akin to Hattie Jacques's roles as matron in the famous 'Carry On' films - very regimental and strict. The first series ran for seven episodes and, although Doris Hare is widely regarded as the Mrs Butler, Cicely Courtneidge made a significant contribution to the On The Buses success story.

It was in 1972 that Cicely Courtneidge was bestowed with the title of Dame Commander of the British Empire (DBE) for her services to theatre following on from her CBE in 1951. Her final show business performance was in the British comedy film Not Now, Darling in 1973.

At the age of 87 Cicely Courtneidge died of natural causes in London on 26th April 1980 after a show business career that lasted for over 60 years.

Filmography

Film

The Ghost Train (1931)
Happy Ever After (1932)
Jack's the Boy (1932)
Falling for You (1933)
Aunt Sally (1933)
Soldiers of the King (1934)
Things Are Looking Up (1935)
Me and Marlborough (1935)
The Perfect Gentleman (1935)
Everybody Dance (1936)
Take My Tip (1937)
Under Your Heart (1940)
Miss Tulip Stays the Night (1955)
The Spider's Web (1960)
The L-Shaped Room (1962)
Those Magnificent Men in Their Flying Machines (1965)
The Wrong Box (1966)
Not Now, Darling (1973)

Television

Kraft Mystery Theatre (1961)
Man of the World (1963)
Before the Fringe (1967)
On The Buses (1969)

On The Buses
A Brief Synopsis

The On The Buses plotline focused on a working-class family and life at the Luxton and District Traction Company in the late 1960s and early 1970s. The Butler family consisted of bus driver Stan Butler, who loved to flout the rules at work and wind up the Inspector; his dowdy, unemployed sister Olive Rudge; know-it-all, snobbish brother-in-law Arthur Rudge; and interfering and fiercely protective mother Mabel Butler.

Stan Butler's career as a bus driver for Luxton and District Traction Company is filled with mishaps, alongside his best mate Jack Harper, who as shop steward often has to dig them out of trouble. Always diligent is their boss Inspector Blake, who is constantly pulling them up for their unpunctuality, scruffiness, flirtatious behaviour with the female conductors (better known as 'clippies') and use of company property without permission. There is an intense rivalry between the two mischievous busmen and Inspector Blake, which makes for a hilarious situation comedy.

On the home front there is constant friction between Stan and Arthur, who both take great pleasure in winding each other up. Marital bliss it certainly is not for Arthur and Olive, who constantly have sly digs at one another, and this situation is further exacerbated by mum, who always has something to say, again making the perfect recipe for classic comedy over the seven series and seventy-four episodes.

EPISODE SYNOPSIS

Series 1, Episode 1 – 'The Early Shift'
Written by Ronald Wolfe and Ronald Chesney
Original Transmission: Friday 28th February 1969 at 7.30 p.m.

Stan has been given a brand new work schedule, which causes problems. Early shifts mean that no canteen facilities are available for him or his work colleagues - much to Blakey's delight. The situation gets out of hand and the bus crews go on unofficial strike at the Luxton and District Traction Company.

The strike affects everyone and the Butlers and Rudges find that the going gets tough, as Stan will get no strike pay and the family is left with no bus service to get them home from the shops. Stan is also called upon for early picket-line duty, but things look up when a television crew turns up at the depot, giving the strike much-needed publicity. However, further drama ensues when a bus attempts to leave the depot.

Will the strike achieve its end goal or will the bus crews have to stick to the new shifts?

CAST:

Stan	Reg Varney
Mum	Cicely Courtneidge
Arthur	Michael Robbins
Olive	Anna Karen
Jack	Bob Grant
Inspector	Stephen Lewis
TV Interviewer	Fraser Kerr
George	Rudolph Walker
Lofty	John M. East
TV Newsman	Kevin Moore

TV Newsman	Michael Slater
DESIGNER:	David Catley
PRODUCED AND DIRECTED BY:	Stuart Allen

Series 1, Episode 2 – 'The New Conductor'
Written by Ronald Wolfe and Ronald Chesney
Original Transmission: Friday 7th March 1969 at 7.30 p.m.

Stan is to have a new conductor aboard his bus and this always makes him nervous. He worries about their competency to such an extent that he feels unwell. However, there is a definite improvement in his health when his new conductor turns out to be an attractive clippie called Iris. The pair get on so well together that they go out on a date after their shift.

Problems arise, though, as Stan has to get out of taking his mum to bingo by pretending that he has to work overtime. After his date he brings Iris home but his mum is not happy and does her best to scupper any chance for romance between Stan and Iris. Mum interrupts just as things are heating up between the pair, offering cocoa and kipper sandwiches - a sure passion killer. What are the chances of romance for Stan?

CAST:

Stan	Reg Varney
Mum	Cicely Courtneidge
Arthur	Michael Robbins
Olive	Anna Karen
Iris	Gwendolyn Watts
Jack	Bob Grant
Inspector	Stephen Lewis

DESIGNER: David Catley
PRODUCED AND DIRECTED BY: Stuart Allen

Series 1, Episode 3 – 'Olive Takes A Trip'
Written by Ronald Wolfe and Ronald Chesney
Original Transmission: Friday 14th March 1969 at 7.30 p.m.

Olive has never been able to hold down a job, so brother Stan is shocked to hear that she is going to apply for a job as a bus conductor at the depot. He insists that she has no chance of getting the job and is even more adamant when he discovers that his mum and Olive are being less than truthful when filling in the application form.

When Olive's application is accepted, Stan is put upon to help his sister out and mum insists that both he and Arthur act as mock customers at home as Olive prepares for her first shift, but this means that they have to miss a football match on TV. Things get worse for Stan when his mum makes arrangements with Inspector Blake for Olive to work her first shift aboard Stan's bus. Is Stan worrying unnecessarily? Only time will tell.

CAST:

Stan	Reg Varney
Mum	Cicely Courtneidge
Arthur	Michael Robbins
Olive	Anna Karen
Jack	Bob Grant
Inspector	Stephen Lewis
Old Gentleman	Geoffrey Denton
Irate Passenger	Terry Duggan
Family Man	Michael Slater

DESIGNER: David Catley
PRODUCED AND DIRECTED BY: Stuart Allen

Series 1, Episode 4 – 'Bus Driver's Stomach'
Written by Ronald Wolfe and Ronald Chesney
Original Transmission: Friday 21st March 1969 at 7.30 p.m.

Stan's recurring stomach pains leave him open to ridicule from Arthur. He insists that Stan's poor diet of greasy chips, chips and yet more chips are the reason for his stomach troubles. Stan disagrees, describing his ailment as an old work-related condition called 'bus driver's stomach', caused by sitting over the engine and thus making his job an occupational hazard. Mum listens to Arthur quoting from a book about the possible seriousness of Stan's problem and decides to put him on a diet.

At the bus depot the management are also clamping down on unfit drivers by transferring them to cleaning or maintenance work, which worries Stan. It is also announced that all drivers are to undergo a medical to prove their fitness.

A visit out of the blue from his doctor catches Stan unawares and after an examination he is put on a strict diet. But will Stan be able to stick to it? He will have to if he wants to pass the medical and keep his job.

CAST:

Stan	Reg Varney
Mum	Cicely Courtneidge
Arthur	Michael Robbins
Olive	Anna Karen
Jack	Bob Grant
Inspector	Stephen Lewis
Doctor Clark	Richard Caldicot
Harry	Arthur Lovegrove
Bert	Nosher Powell

DESIGNER: Andrew Gardner
PRODUCED AND DIRECTED BY: Stuart Allen

Series 1, Episode 5 – 'The New Inspector'
Written by Ronald Wolfe and Ronald Chesney
Original Transmission: Friday 28th March 1969 at 7.30 p.m.

A Bus Inspector vacancy becomes available at the depot, but the post is seen as a poisoned chaliced by Stan and Jack. It is hard to imagine any driver or conductor taking on the role, but financially the post is rewarding.

When Stan gets home to see his mum patching up her old coat in preparation for a night out and knowing that she would love to buy a new coat, he realises that with a few extra pounds in wages he could treat his mum to the coat of her dreams. Stan decides to take the plunge and apply for the post of Inspector.

Interest in the job is minimal and Stan takes on the new role, but he soon sees a change in attitudes towards him from his workmates. He is shunned and insulted and, to make matters worse, he is demoted from the bus depot's darts team. Stan has problems elsewhere when carrying out his new duties and something must give.

CAST:

Stan	Reg Varney
Mum	Cicely Courtneidge
Arthur	Michael Robbins
Olive	Anna Karen
Jack	Bob Grant
Inspector	Stephen Lewis
Betty	Doreen Herrington
Manager	Arnold Peters
Jenny	Valerie Newbold

DESIGNER: Andrew Gardner
PRODUCED AND DIRECTED BY: Stuart Allen

Series 1, Episode 6 – 'The Canteen'
Written by Ronald Wolfe and Ronald Chesney
Original Transmission: Friday 4th April 1969 at 7.30 p.m.

There is great jubilation amongst the staff at the bus depot when it is announced that the management have agreed to let them run the depot's canteen. Shop Steward Jack places Stan in charge, much to his surprise. His first task is to appoint a cook and he believes he has found the solution when a colleague puts forward his wife for the job, telling Stan she is an experienced cook having worked in a similar post. He employs her immediately.

Stan is in for a shock though, as the cook cannot speak a word of English and doesn't cook the sort of food the bus crews crave. The Indian woman has come straight from a job working for Bombay Buses and cooks spicy curry and tea made in the Indian style. Blakey takes great pleasure in Stan's discomfort, as his work colleagues are far from pleased with matters. It is obvious that things aren't working out, so Stan looks closer to home for help.

CAST:

Stan	Reg Varney
Mum	Cicely Courtneidge
Arthur	Michael Robbins
Olive	Anna Karen
Jack	Bob Grant
Inspector	Stephen Lewis
Bert	Nosher Powell
Mrs Sharma	Shiranee Fullerton
Mr Sharma	Mohammad Shamsi

DESIGNER: Andrew Gardner
PRODUCED AND DIRECTED BY: Stuart Allen

Series 1, Episode 7 – 'The Darts Match'
Written by Ronald Wolfe and Ronald Chesney
Original Transmission: Friday 11th April 1969 at 7.30 p.m.

When two clippies commandeer the dartboard in the canteen Stan and Jack are not too happy. One of the clippies is an old flame of Stan's and she and her friend don't take kindly to being ushered off the board. It all ends with their challenging Stan and Jack to a darts match and they are so confident of winning that they put a wager on the result.

Stan's preparations for the big match, however, are to be severely hampered. His favourite set of darts are ruined when one ends up in Olive's stew as he practices at home. It is also a distraction to him that one of his opponents is Iris and he arranges a date with her, which doesn't go down well with Jack or his mum.

When the battle-of-the-sexes darts match gets under way the dirty tricks begin and may the best man or woman win.

CAST:

Stan	Reg Varney
Mum	Cicely Courtneidge
Arthur	Michael Robbins
Olive	Anna Karen
Jack	Bob Grant
Inspector	Stephen Lewis
Iris	Gwendolyn Watts
Jenny	Valerie Newbold

DESIGNER: Andrew Gardner
PRODUCED AND DIRECTED BY: Stuart Allen

Series 2, Episode 1 – 'Family Flu'
Written by Ronald Wolfe and Ronald Chesney
Original Transmission: Saturday 31st May 1969 at 7.00 p.m.

When Olive and mum are bedridden with flu it is left to Stan and Arthur to do all of the housework. Stan's cooking leaves a lot to be desired and Arthur takes on the washing-up. The shopping has to be done by Stan while he is on a shift, which doesn't amuse Blakey, and things get worse when Arthur also becomes victim to the flu, leaving Stan to cope all on his own.

Stan has to take everyone's washing to the launderette, which leads to his landing himself in more trouble with Blakey and leaves him open to ridicule from Jack and the Inspector. Perhaps there is light at the end of the tunnel for Stan, as the invalid's mum, Olive and Arthur are going away to visit a relative. But life is very cruel to Stan and he won't find things getting any easier.

CAST:

Stan	Reg Varney
Mum	Doris Hare
Arthur	Michael Robbins
Olive	Anna Karen
Jack	Bob Grant
Inspector	Stephen Lewis

DESIGNER: Andrew Gardner
PRODUCED AND DIRECTED BY: Stuart Allen

Series 2, Episode 2 – 'The Used Combination'
Written by Ronald Wolfe and Ronald Chesney
Original Transmission: Saturday 7th June 1969 at 7.00 p.m.

Arthur buys himself a second-hand motorbike combination that is a little worse for wear. When showing it off to the family he lays himself open to a great deal of criticism from Stan, especially as the seatbelt breaks, the tyres are flat, it has an inadequate tool kit and it fails to start despite all Arthur's efforts. When Stan breaks off the starter he is told that he'll have to fix it, forcing him to smuggle tools out of the bus depot.

After repairs are completed Arthur decides to go out on a test run with mum in the sidecar and Olive riding pillion. The inevitable happens, with the motorbike breaking down miles from home. Luckily, Stan's bus passes by and so he tows the bike behind the bus, but another mishap then occurs: the handlebars break off. So Stan finds himself in a spot of bother when he gets back to the depot, as he has to explain away the presence of a tow rope and handlebars dangling from the back of his bus to Inspector Blake.

CAST:

Stan	Reg Varney
Mum	Doris Hare
Arthur	Michael Robbins
Olive	Anna Karen
Jack	Bob Grant
Inspector	Stephen Lewis

DESIGNER: Andrew Gardner
PRODUCED AND DIRECTED BY: Stuart Allen

Series 2, Episode 3 – 'Self-Defence'
Written by Ronald Wolfe and Ronald Chesney
Original Transmission: Saturday 14th June 1969 at 7.00 p.m.

Saturday night shifts are proving hazardous for Stan and Jack, as another shift ends with their being assaulted and the bus vandalised by football hooligans and other undesirables. They demand that they are given protection and refuse to take buses out late in the evening.

Luxton and District Traction Company puts in place a course of self-defence lessons, which are to be given by Inspector Blake. Stan and Jack feel it's all a waste of time until they see an attractive pair of clippies sign up for the classes, resulting in a swift change of opinion.

The lessons turn out to be a very painful experience for Stan. Blakey demonstrates some moves on Stan and then gets a clippie who has studied judo to display her skills on the hapless driver, leaving him flat out. He realises that, despite Jack's romantic notions, he wouldn't risk anything with her. The pain doesn't end there for Stan, as he is to suffer more agony at home.

CAST:

Stan	Reg Varney
Mum	Doris Hare
Arthur	Michael Robbins
Olive	Anna Karen
Jack	Bob Grant
Inspector	Stephen Lewis
Joyce	Avril Gaynor
Liz	Ursula Mohan

DESIGNER: Andrew Gardner
PRODUCED AND DIRECTED BY: Stuart Allen

Series 2, Episode 4 – 'Aunt Maud'
Written by Ronald Wolfe and Ronald Chesney
Original Transmission: Saturday 21st June 1969 at 7.00 p.m.

The Butlers get a family visit from Aunt Maud, which inevitably leads to problems for Stan. He is caught by the Inspector detouring from his set route to pick up his aunt and gets a ticking-off for allowing her large pet dog on the bus.

Living arrangements at the Butlers are also disrupted by Aunt Maud's arrival, with Stan having to give up his bed and share with Arthur, which doesn't go down at all well. Stan, Arthur and Olive also have to go through an embarrassing third-degree, as Maud asks her sister why Arthur and Olive haven't started a family and why Stan has never married. Trying to share a bed with Arthur proves too much for Stan and he ends up spending the night sleeping downstairs.

Aunt Maud's departure doesn't go smoothly either, as Stan has to try to smuggle her dog onto the bus in order to see that she gets back home and he in turn gets his bedroom back.

CAST:

Stan	Reg Varney
Mum	Doris Hare
Arthur	Michael Robbins
Olive	Anna Karen
Jack	Bob Grant
Inspector	Stephen Lewis
Aunt Maud	Betty Hare

DESIGNER: Andrew Gardner
PRODUCED AND DIRECTED BY: Stuart Allen

Series 2, Episode 5 – 'Late Again'

Written by Ronald Wolfe and Ronald Chesney

Original Transmission: Saturday 28th June 1969 at 7.00 p.m.

Stan's love life and early-morning shifts just don't mix. He is out until the early hours with his girlfriend and finds getting up at 5 a.m. for work an impossible task. His alarm wakes up Arthur but he's still dead to the world and so arrives late for work. Fortunately, Jack saves his skin and forges his signature to sign him in on time.

Arthur is fed up of being woken up by Stan's alarm clock and decides to adjust the volume to make it quieter. As a result, Stan is once more late for work. Unfortunately, this time Blakey is on patrol and Stan is forced to enter the depot via the men's toilet window. By mistake, however, he clambers through the wrong window and finds himself in the women's toilet, startling a clippie, and lands himself in trouble with Blakey.

The problem is solved when Blakey moves Stan onto late shifts, but how will this affect his love life?

CAST:

Stan	Reg Varney
Mum	Doris Hare
Arthur	Michael Robbins
Olive	Anna Karen
Jack	Bob Grant
Inspector	Stephen Lewis
Doreen	Kate Williams
Ada	Sue Walker

DESIGNER: Andrew Gardner

PRODUCED AND DIRECTED BY: Stuart Allen

Series 2, Episode 6 – 'Bon Voyage'
Written by Ronald Wolfe and Ronald Chesney
Original Transmission: Saturday 5th July 1969 at 7.00 p.m.

The bus depot's staff holiday to Spain is nearing and Stan and Jack are preparing for it in various ways. They demonstrate to a bemused Blakey their ploy of attracting señoritas as they pose as photographers. Also, in an attempt to buff up their suntans, they take to sunbathing in the cemetery's graveyard, but a passing tramp helps himself to Stan's uniform and he has to drive the bus partially dressed. On his return to the depot he is told that he will have to pay for a new uniform, thus depriving him of his holiday spending money.

Stan has to be careful when packing for his holiday in order to avoid any excess baggage charges, so he weighs his luggage individually and Olive adds up the total, aided in the end by Arthur. It becomes clear that he won't be able to take everything he wants, but he finds a way around the problem even if it is uncomfortable.

CAST:

Stan	Reg Varney
Mum	Doris Hare
Arthur	Michael Robbins
Olive	Anna Karen
Jack	Bob Grant
Inspector	Stephen Lewis
Eileen	Sally Douglas
Nobby	Patrick Connor

GRAPHICS BY:	Terry Griffiths
DESIGNER:	Andrew Gardner
PRODUCED AND DIRECTED BY:	Stuart Allen

Series 3, Episode 1 – 'First Aid'
Written by Ronald Wolfe and Ronald Chesney
Original Transmission: Friday 2nd January 1970 at 8.30 p.m.

Inspector Blake has an accident when aboard Stan's bus and it is left to Stan and Jack to administer first aid after he slips on their chips. They find Blakey with a cut shin and twisted knee, but their attempts at treatment only make matters worse and an inadequate on-board first-aid box doesn't help. However, relief is at hand when they return to the depot.

As a result of this unfortunate incident the management decide that all staff must pass a first-aid test and Stan and Jack are chosen as the first candidates. With only a day to swot up on the subject, Stan has to get brother-in-law Arthur and his sister Olive to help him with his revision. Will their assistance be of any use in his bid to avoid being moved to cleaning or maintenance should he fail his first-aid test? Also how would Stan react in an emergency aboard his bus?

CAST:

Stan	Reg Varney
Mum	Doris Hare
Jack	Bob Grant
Arthur	Michael Robbins
Inspector	Stephen Lewis
Olive	Anna Karen
Nurse	Ruth Kettlewell
Eileen	Suzanne Vasey

DESIGNER: Roger Hall
PRODUCED AND DIRECTED BY: Stuart Allen

Series 3, Episode 2 – 'The Cistern'
Written by Ronald Wolfe and Ronald Chesney
Original Transmission: Friday 9th January 1970 at 8.30 p.m.

When the terrible post-flush noises made by the Butlers toilet cistern become too annoying Stan decides to do some plumbing. However, instead of solving the problem he proceeds to ruin Arthur's torch and crack the toilet basin, making it totally unusable.

After some debate the family club together to buy a brand new cistern, basin and pipes, but they are confronted by more problems. To cut costs they decide to avoid delivery charges and take their purchase home on the bus, but they run into Inspector Blake en route. Also they attempt to do the plumbing themselves.

It's all down to Stan to fit the new toilet, but just when it looks as though he's done a great job it becomes clear that another problem needs resolving.

CAST:

Stan	Reg Varney
Mum	Doris Hare
Arthur	Michael Robbins
Olive	Anna Karen
Jack	Bob Grant
Inspector	Stephen Lewis
Shopkeeper	Terry Duggan

DESIGNER: Roger Hall
PRODUCED AND DIRECTED BY: Stuart Allen

Series 3, Episode 3 – 'The Inspector's Niece'
Written by Ronald Wolfe and Ronald Chesney
Original Transmission: Friday 16th January 1970 at 8.30 p.m.

Stan and Jack are flung into direct competition when they both fall for their latest trainee clippie. Both will need to clean up their act to impress her, however, as she hates unhygienic, scruffy men. This prompts Stan to race home during his lunch break so that he can wash, shave and have his uniform ironed. Meanwhile, Jack uses the opportunity to change from a sweater into a loud, floral shirt and matching tie.

The afternoon shift sees Stan and Jack vying to win the new clippie's affections. Jack's dress sense and sense of humour seem to be winning her over, but Stan isn't giving up. He prevents Jack from giving her flowers by shutting the doors of the bus as he is about to board, leaving him to run after the bus in order to catch up with them at the Cemetery Gates.

What Stan and Jack don't realise is that the trainee clippie is Inspector Blake's niece, Sally.

CAST:

Stan	Reg Varney
Mum	Doris Hare
Arthur	Michael Robbins
Olive	Anna Karen
Jack	Bob Grant
Inspector	Stephen Lewis
Sally	Madeleine Mills
Gladys	Parnell McGarry

DESIGNER	Andrew Gardner
PRODUCED AND DIRECTED BY	Stuart Allen

Series 3, Episode 4 – 'Brew It Yourself'

Written by Ronald Wolfe and Ronald Chesney
Original Transmission: Friday 23rd January 1970 at 8.30 p.m.

Stan tries his hand at brewing his own beer, but who will be brave enough to try some? It turns out to be very much to his liking, but mum, Arthur and Olive are sceptical and so Stan samples the drinks for them before returning to the bus depot for his shift. Little does he know just how strong his beer actually is, but he is soon going to find out.

Stan arrives at the depot drunk and Inspector Blake sees it as a great chance to get rid of him for good. Blakey demands that Stan should take a breathalyser test and warns him that if it proves positive he will be sacked. Shop Steward and best friend Jack is on hand to try all the tricks in the book to save Stan from dismissal, which include forcing him to eat several platefuls of mashed potato and breathing smoke into the breathalyser. It is just a matter of time before Stan knows whether or not he has lost his job.

CAST:

Stan	Reg Varney
Mum	Doris Hare
Arthur	Michael Robbins
Olive	Anna Karen
Jack	Bob Grant
Inspector	Stephen Lewis
Susie	Sally Douglas
Chalkie	Glen Whitter

DESIGNER: Andrew Gardner
PRODUCED AND DIRECTED BY: Stuart Allen

Series 3, Episode 5 – 'Busmen's Perks'
Written by Ronald Wolfe and Ronald Chesney
Original Transmission: Friday 30th January 1970 at 8.30 p.m.

Arthur insists that his bedroom needs redecorating, describing it as 'unfit for human habitation'. He does have a point, as damp is causing the wallpaper to peel off and mould adorns the ceiling. He manages to enlist Stan's help, saying that otherwise he will bring in professional decorators, which will be expensive. Stan tells him that he can get hold of some cheap paint from the bus depot and they will paint the bedroom.

First of all Stan has to smuggle the paint out of the depot, which proves to be a very uncomfortable experience for him. Painting the bedroom is also fraught with problems, as Arthur forgets to put the hardener in the paint, meaning it takes even longer to dry. There are more fun and games when Olive needs to pay a visit to the toilet in the middle of the night surrounded by wet paint, and it all ends with things getting very painful for Arthur.

CAST:

Stan	Reg Varney
Mum	Doris Hare
Arthur	Michael Robbins
Olive	Anna Karen
Jack	Bob Grant
The Inspector	Stephen Lewis
Nobby	Norman Mitchell
Janet	Lynn Dalby

DESIGNER: Andrew Gardner
PRODUCED AND DIRECTED BY: Stuart Allen

Series 3, Episode 6 – 'The Snake'
Written by Ronald Wolfe and Ronald Chesney
Original Transmission: Friday 6th February 1970 at 8.30 p.m.

There is an Indian social event at the bus depot and the canteen cook, whom Stan and Jack have both taken a shine to, performs an artistic dance with her pet snake. At the end of the evening it is Jack who wins a date with Fatima, but Stan thinks he has had the last laugh when she insists on taking her pet with her on the date. As Stan is about to go home Jack gives him his laundry bag to take back with him. Unaware that the bag contains more than just clothes, Stan brings an uninvited guest into the Butler house.

The snake finds its way out of the bag and is on the loose and the family are forced to take refuge in the bathroom. Mum shouts for help out of the window, but will anyone come to their rescue? Finally help is at hand when Jack and Fatima pay them a visit.

CAST:

Stan	Reg Varney
Mum	Doris Hare
Arthur	Michael Robbins
Olive	Anna Karen
The Inspector	Stephen Lewis
Jack	Bob Grant
Fatima	Julia Mendez
Ahmed	Ishaq Bux
Vina Player	Vemu Makunda
Tabla Player	Austin Baptiste

DESIGNER: Andrew Gardner
PRODUCED AND DIRECTED BY: Stuart Allen

Series 3, Episode 7 – 'Mum's Last Fling'
Written by Ronald Wolfe and Ronald Chesney
Original Transmission: Friday 13th February 1970 at 8.30 p.m.

Bills are going unpaid and Mrs Butler is leaving the housework to Olive, which means that Stan and Arthur have to put up with Olive's cooking. It becomes clear where all the housekeeping money is going, as mum has found herself a boyfriend and treats herself to a new coat, wig and thigh-length boots to impress him and experiences her new lease of life.

His mum's choice of boyfriend leaves Stan feeling uneasy, as he is a bus conductor with a reputation. Things get worse when he pays the Butlers a visit and suggests that mum could make a lot of money by moving the family out and renting out the rooms to lodgers. Fed up of having to wash and iron his shirts, Stan and Arthur are determined to scupper mum's romance. Stan unearths some details about him and someone is bound to get hurt by the revelations.

CAST:

Stan	Reg Varney
Mum	Doris Hare
Arthur	Michael Robbins
Olive	Anna Karen
Jack	Bob Grant
The Inspector	Stephen Lewis
Wilfred	Tommy Godfrey
The Traffic Warden	Eunice Black
The Commissionaire	Frank Littlewood

DESIGNER: Andrew Gardner
PRODUCED AND DIRECTED BY: Stuart Allen

Series 3, Episode 8 – 'Radio Control'
Written by Ronald Wolfe and Ronald Chesney
Original Transmission: Friday 20th February 1970 at 8.30 p.m.

The Luxton and District Traction Company decide to tackle the problem of delays on their buses by having each bus fitted with a two-way radio system. The first bus to have the system installed will be Stan and Jack's No. 11 to the Cemetery Gates due to their constant unpunctuality.

This move means that Stan has to learn a code and has to revise it at home, much to the displeasure of the family, but other problems exist. The system will also hamper Stan and Jack's efforts to do as they please, especially when two clippies are put on their bus for training purposes.

Something must give, and when they arrive at the Cemetery Gates Stan and Jack decide to have some fun with the clippies, but are disturbed too often by Inspector Blake over the airwaves. When Blakey turns up en route to check up on them he gives Stan orders that he later regrets and ends up paying the price.

CAST:

Stan	Reg Varney
Mum	Doris Hare
Arthur	Michael Robbins
Olive	Anna Karen
Jack	Bob Grant
The Inspector	Stephen Lewis
The Pilot	Fraser Kerr
Edna	Patricia Clapton
The Radio Girl	Valerie Newbold
Joyce	Ursula Mohan

DESIGNER: Andrew Gardner
PRODUCED AND DIRECTED BY: Stuart Allen

Series 3, Episode 9 – 'Foggy Night'
Written by Ronald Wolfe and Ronald Chesney
Original Transmission: Friday 27th February 1970 at 8.30 p.m.

The family decide to pay a visit to Aunt Maud and travel there on Stan's bus, with the Inspector also aboard keeping his eye on Stan and Jack. In the evening they pick up mum, Arthur and Olive for the return journey just as a thick fog is beginning to roll in.

Hazardous driving conditions force Stan to call a halt to the journey as the fog continues to thicken. The passengers are forced to settle down for a long night aboard the bus, but Olive causes problems when she needs to go to the toilet and a trip out into the foggy night sees her getting in a pickle. There is also trouble in store for Blakey when he makes an effort to guide the bus out of the fog.

Being stranded in the fog overnight sees Blakey suffer more torment from Stan and Jack even when he is asleep. Still they see it as a way to entertain themselves until the fog lifts.

CAST:

Stan	Reg Varney
Mum	Doris Hare
Arthur	Michael Robbins
Olive	Anna Karen
Jack	Bob Grant
The Inspector	Stephen Lewis
The Woman Passenger	Katherine Page
Disc Jockey	Pete Brady

DESIGNER: Andrew Gardner
PRODUCED AND DIRECTED BY: Stuart Allen

Series 3, Episode 10 – 'The New Uniforms'
Written by Ronald Wolfe and Ronald Chesney
Original Transmission: Friday 6th March 1970 at 8.30 p.m.

As the scruffiest busmen in the depot, Stan and Jack are chosen to model the proposed new uniforms. Even the pictures of the new uniforms look hilarious to them, but there is even more hilarity when they don the uniforms for the first time. Stan and Jack take to a makeshift catwalk in the canteen to model the uniforms and must take a lot of flak from their workmates, as they now look more like Peruvian postmen than busmen.

Matters are made worse by Inspector Blake, who watches Stan and Jack's every move and tries to prevent them from dirtying their uniforms while eating in the canteen. As a result they decide to go elsewhere to eat and it is then that they bump into a couple of young Swedish women who mistake them for airline pilots because of their new attire. All of a sudden the uniforms take on a new light for Stan and Jack and they are happy to wear them as they appear to impress the fairer sex, but will their enthusiasm last?

CAST:

Stan	Reg Varney
Mum	Doris Hare
Arthur	Michael Robbins
Olive	Anna Karen
Jack	Bob Grant
The Inspector	Stephen Lewis
Ingrid	Yutte Stensgaard
Birgit	Pauline Cunningham
The Clippie	Elyse Clare
Chalkie	Glen Whitter

DESIGNER: Andrew Gardner
PRODUCED AND DIRECTED BY: Stuart Allen

Series 3, Episode 11 – 'Going Steady'
Written by Ronald Wolfe and Ronald Chesney
Original Transmission: Friday 13th March 1970 at 8.30 p.m.

Stan has been dating Sally for some time, but the clippie happens to be the Inspector's niece. In order to maximise the chances of the relationship going any further Stan makes a number of sacrifices and there is a noticeable change in his attitude and dress sense.

Stan proclaims that he has given up smoking, but in reality it is only when Sally is around. When he tells Blakey about his intention to marry her the Inspector is far from happy. Stan won't be put off and in an attempt to win him over he invites Blakey and Sally to tea, and even crawls by promising that his bus will leave on time. Jack is affected as well, as he is pushed aside and is replaced by Sally as Stan's conductor.

The Butlers make an effort to impress when Blakey and Sally come to tea, especially Stan. However, will mum take to Sally's snobbish attitude and criticism of Stan and can he and Blakey really get on over tea? Time will tell.

CAST:

Stan	Reg Varney
Mum	Doris Hare
Arthur	Michael Robbins
Olive	Anna Karen
Jack	Bob Grant
The Inspector	Stephen Lewis
Sally	Madeleine Mills

DESIGNER:	Andrew Gardner
PRODUCED BY:	Stuart Allen
DIRECTED BY:	Howard Ross

Series 3, Episode 12 – 'The Squeeze'
Written by Ronald Wolfe and Ronald Chesney
Original Transmission: Friday 20th March 1970 at 8.30 p.m.

The Butler household is suffering a financial crisis and they don't even have sufficient money to pay the milkman. Mum is demanding more housekeeping money from Stan and Arthur, which they cannot afford, and so Stan suggests that Arthur should sell his precious motorbike to raise some cash. Composing an advert for the motorbike proves to be difficult, as it is in such poor condition: covered in rust and it won't even start.

The advert is placed on the noticeboard at the bus depot, but it fails to raise any interest, so Stan and Jack try convincing Blakey that the motorbike is just what he needs. They even offer him the chance of a test ride in the sidecar before he makes a decision. This means that the family have a lot of work to do preparing the motorbike for its trip and Stan uses all the tricks in the book to ensure that the bike sounds healthy and survives the test journey. Will Blakey be convinced to buy the motorbike or will the Butlers remain in their financial crisis?

CAST:

Stan	Reg Varney
Mum	Doris Hare
Arthur	Michael Robbins
Olive	Anna Karen
Jack	Bob Grant
The Inspector	Stephen Lewis
Chalkie	Glen Whitter
The Milkman	Mike Carnell
DESIGNER:	Andrew Gardner
PRODUCER:	Stuart Allen
DIRECTOR:	Howard Ross

Series 3, Episode 13 – 'On The Make'
Written by Ronald Wolfe and Ronald Chesney
Original Transmission: Friday 27th March 1970 at 8.30 p.m.

When one of the clippies, Edna, is flung out of her accommodation and left homeless Stan is on hand to help out. He tells that her she can move into the Butlers' spare room and, despite Arthur's objections, the family agree to take her as a lodger.

Stan bends over backwards to help Edna by picking up her cases, which turns out to be a lot of baggage. He also agrees to take her pet dog back to the Butlers, but he soon wishes he hadn't when the dog turns out to be extremely large and troublesome.

Edna moves into Stan's room and he is forced to sleep downstairs in the front room. He now has to work out how to get into her room without the family finding out, which won't be easy as Arthur is aware of Stan's plan and is determined to block his attempts. However, Stan doesn't give up and even tries to use Edna's dog to lure her downstairs into his arms.

CAST:

Stan	Reg Varney
Mum	Doris Hare
Arthur	Michael Robbins
Olive	Anna Karen
Jack	Bob Grant
The Inspector	Stephen Lewis
Edna	Patricia Clapton

DESIGNER:	Andrew Gardner
PRODUCER:	Stuart Allen
DIRECTOR:	Howard Ross

Series 4, Episode 1 – 'Nowhere To Go'
Written by Ronald Wolfe and Ronald Chesney
Original Transmission: Friday 27th November 1970 at 8.30 p.m.

Stan and Jack are dating two clippies, but they are having problems finding somewhere they can get amorous with them. The Butler house is out of bounds due to the nosiness of the family and even their attempts to use the bus for their courting are foiled by Blakey.

The following day might see Stan's luck change, as Arthur, Olive and mum are planning to visit Aunt Maud. However, they intend travelling aboard Arthur's motorbike combination and he can't get it started, so Stan is eager to help him. More obstacles stand in the way when Arthur and Olive get cold feet about the trip, and then as they finally leave the motorbike's front wheel snaps off. Stan refuses to give up on the idea of having the house to himself for courting, so he makes an attempt to repair Arthur's bike at the depot's maintenance department, but all does not go to plan.

CAST:

Stan	Reg Varney
Mum	Doris Hare
Arthur	Michael Robbins
Olive	Anna Karen
Jack	Bob Grant
The Inspector	Stephen Lewis
Suzy	Suzanne Heath
Edna	Ursula Mohan
Joe	Eric Francis
The Cleaner	Ian Gray

DESIGNER:	Alan Hunter-Craig
PRODUCER:	Stuart Allen

Series 4, Episode 2 – 'The Canteen Girl'
Written by Ronald Wolfe and Ronald Chesney
Original Transmission: Friday 4th December 1970 at 8.30 p.m.

Everyone is happy at the bus depot, including Inspector Blake. He is dating the canteen cook, Molly, and he plans to ask her to move away to the countryside so that they can run a farm together. This is music to Stan and Jack's ears, as they imagine having an easy life without their nemesis ordering them around.

It is announced that Inspector Blake is to leave the depot, but Stan and Jack's joy on hearing the news is short-lived. They are introduced to Blakey's replacement, Inspector Stewart, whose first duty sees him suspend them for their appearance and the state of their bus. The only option open to them is to try to prevent Blakey from leaving and this will mean having to break up his relationship with Molly.

Stan and Jack get Molly drunk before she meets Blakey at the depot for a social event. When he finds her aboard one of the buses trying to get amorous with Stan fireworks are sure to fly and Blakey promises to make Stan's life a misery.

CAST:

Stan	Reg Varney
Mum	Doris Hare
Jack	Bob Grant
The Inspector	Stephen Lewis
Arthur	Michael Robbins
Olive	Anna Karen
Molly	Gaye Brown
Mr Stewart	Alan Curtis

DESIGNER:	Alan Hunter-Craig
PRODUCER:	Stuart Allen

Series 4, Episode 3 – 'Dangerous Driving'
Written by Ronald Wolfe and Ronald Chesney
Original Transmission: Friday 11th December 1970 at 8.30 p.m.

A newspaper article about the health of busmen paints a gloomy picture, claiming that their job is dangerous and reduces their life expectancy. Stan ridicules the article as he lines up another date with a clippie, but his mum is concerned.

Stan decides to kill two birds with one stone. He starts attending the keep-fit classes at the bus depot run by Inspector Blake. First and foremost he sees it as an opportunity to get fit for his date, but it also gives him a chance to appease his family and ease his own growing concerns.

In one of the keep-fit classes Stan finds himself in an uncomfortable exercise with a less than glamorous clippie. He also gets into a contest with Blakey, which sees him losing a bet to the Inspector, and to make matters worse his family place him on a diet.

However, Jack has some good news for Stan that will end his health worries, but he still intends to stay fit for his date.

CAST:

Stan	Reg Varney
Mum	Doris Hare
Arthur	Michael Robbins
Jack	Bob Grant
The Inspector	Stephen Lewis
Olive	Anna Karen
Pat	Clare Sutcliffe
Rosie	Eunice Black
Joe	Derek Carpenter
DESIGNER:	Alan Hunter-Craig
PRODUCER:	Stuart Allen

Series 4, Episode 4 – 'The Other Woman'
Written by Ronald Wolfe and Ronald Chesney
Original Transmission: Friday 18th December 1970 at 8.30 p.m.

A crisis is about to hit the Butler household. At a darts night at the bus depot Arthur spends all of the evening flirting with off-duty clippie Wendy while Olive watches on. The evening degenerates into a full-scale argument and Olive goes home alone, leaving Arthur to carry on his flirting.

Arthur arrives home in the early hours of the morning to find Olive, mum and Stan waiting for answers. Olive is not happy with what she hears and vows to lock him out of their bedroom, and when the arguments get more heated Arthur walks out.

When the new day dawns Arthur is still missing and Olive is distraught. He walks in as they are having breakfast, but not everything is as it seems: he has only returned to pick up his belongings. Has Olive really lost Arthur to another woman or is there another explanation? All will be revealed at the bus depot.

CAST:

Stan	Reg Varney
Mum	Doris Hare
Arthur	Michael Robbins
Olive	Anna Karen
Jack	Bob Grant
The Inspector	Stephen Lewis
Wendy	Kate Williams
DESIGNER:	Alan Hunter-Craig
PRODUCER:	Stuart Allen

Series 4, Episode 5 – 'Christmas Duty'
Written by Ronald Wolfe and Ronald Chesney
Original Transmission: Friday 25th December 1970 at 8.30 p.m.

It is Christmas Day, but there is no rest for the wicked. Stan and Jack are called in to cover a shift when a crew falls ill. This means that the family's festive celebrations will have to wait until Stan has finished work, but even more problems are on the cards.

At the end of his shift Stan finds himself waiting for ages at the depot for Arthur to pick him up on his motorbike, but Arthur has been celebrating in the pub and is in no fit state to collect him. Olive, who is still a learner, takes over the driving, with Arthur riding pillion and mum in the sidecar - but who is minding the Christmas dinner, which is in the oven?

On arrival at the depot Olive causes chaos, sending Blakey diving out of the way as she struggles to bring the motorbike to a halt. The combination smashes into the side of a bus, but luckily there are no injuries. The real damage is taking place at home, as the Christmas dinner is still cooking and soon becomes ruined. What a Christmas Day for the Butlers.

CAST:

Stan	Reg Varney
Mum	Doris Hare
Jack	Bob Grant
The Inspector	Stephen Lewis
Arthur	Michael Robbins
Olive	Anna Karen
The Policeman	Roger Avon
Joyce	Ursula Mohan
Rosie	Eunice Black
DESIGNER:	Alan Hunter-Craig
PRODUCER:	Stuart Allen

Series 4, Episode 6 – 'The 'L' Bus'
Written by Ronald Wolfe and Ronald Chesney
Original Transmission: Friday 1st January 1971 at 8.30 p.m.

It is Stan and Jack's turn to take out the learner bus and give some training to new staff. Four trainees are under their tuition: two male drivers and two attractive female conductresses. Stan and Jack see this as a chance for more flirting with the opposite sex.

At home, Olive and Arthur are having trouble with their bed and its constant squeaking is keeping the rest of the family awake. Stan's efforts to repair the bed backfire and instead it is completely wrecked. The following morning signals a hunt for a new bed and Jack may have the perfect solution.

Stan, Jack and the trainees use the learner bus to pick up a second-hand bed from a relative of Jack's and stow it on the upper deck, but the bus breaks down. When the bus is towed back to the depot Blakey is on hand to make Stan's life more difficult, as he insists that they take out another bus. The bed remains aboard the learner bus and must be removed, but doing this without Blakey finding out will be no easy task.

CAST:

Stan	Reg Varney
Mum	Doris Hare
Jack	Bob Grant
The Inspector	Stephen Lewis
Arthur	Michael Robbins
Olive	Anna Karen
Bert	John Lyons
Betty	Juel Morrell
Janet	Olivia Breeze
Alf	Reginald Stewart
The Mechanic	Michael Slater
DESIGNER:	Alan Hunter-Craig
PRODUCER:	Stuart Allen

Series 4, Episode 7 – 'The Kids' Outing'
Written by Ronald Wolfe and Ronald Chesney
Original Transmission: Sunday 10th January 1971 at 7.25 p.m.

It's the day of the bus depot's children's outing and Stan has been given the arduous task of driving the bus and organising the whole event. He enlists the help of the family to prepare food and blow up balloons, but will that be enough to keep them entertained? They also have to contend with Blakey's nephew among the children and he brings his own share of trouble with him.

The bus hasn't even left the depot and the children are up to mischief, pouring sugar into the petrol tank. It doesn't take long for the exhaust pipe to fall off and the bus eventually breaks down, forcing them to return to the depot. This doesn't go down well with the kids and they make their displeasure known to Jack, Stan and Blakey.

The children are restless as they wait in the depot canteen for a replacement bus, so in an attempt to keep them entertained Stan dresses up as a clippie. He needn't have bothered, however, as the bus is repaired and the ill-fated kids' outing can continue.

CAST:

Stan	Reg Varney
Mum	Doris Hare
The Inspector	Stephen Lewis
Arthur	Michael Robbins
Olive	Anna Karen
Jack	Bob Grant
Winnie	Winifred Braemar
The Children	Kenneth Flynn
	Keith Garrod
	Sheridan Earl Russell
Bert	John Lyons
Eileen	Doreen Herrington
Bird Impressions by:	Percy Edwards
DESIGNER:	Alan Hunter-Craig
PRODUCER:	Stuart Allen

Series 4, Episode 8 – 'The Anniversary'
Written by Ronald Wolfe and Ronald Chesney
Original Transmission: Sunday 17th January at 7.25 p.m.

It is Olive and Arthur's 10th wedding anniversary, but Stan is certain that Arthur has forgotten. She receives a card from Arthur and is happy, but Stan notices that it is the same card he sent the previous year. The couple also receive an anniversary present from Aunt Maud, which turns out to be a pet dog and this doesn't go down well with Arthur.

Later in the evening the Butlers have a special anniversary dinner and Olive makes a real effort for the occasion. She makes her entrance in a new skirt and hairpiece, which attract raised eyebrows followed by insults. For his part Arthur supplies a bottle of sherry for the dinner, but he is a little less than generous with his measures. During the evening it becomes clear that Arthur has an allergy to their new pet and Olive has accidents with her hairpiece. As things go from bad to worse, it seems to be a night that sums up Arthur and Olive's marriage.

CAST:

Stan	Reg Varney
Mum	Doris Hare
Arthur	Michael Robbins
Olive	Anna Karen
Jack	Bob Grant
The Inspector	Stephen Lewis
The Passenger	Terry Duggan

DESIGNER:	Alan Hunter-Craig
PRODUCER:	Stuart Allen

Series 4, Episode 9 – 'Cover Up'

Written by Ronald Wolfe and Ronald Chesney

Original Transmission: Sunday 24th January 1971 at 7.25 p.m.

The furniture in the Butler household is looking a little worse for wear. There is no denying that re-upholstering the armchair is long overdue, as it is stained with Stan's Brylcream and beneath its cover the stuffing is coming out as well as a spring, but money is in short supply and the Butlers can't afford to pay the phone bill let alone repair the furniture. Stan comes up with an idea on how to make the necessary improvements, which won't cost a penny but will involve risk.

Stan and Jack pay a visit to the maintenance department at the depot and get their hands on a roll of the material used to cover the seats of the buses. They then have to work out how to smuggle the cloth out of the depot without Blakey catching them, and even when they succeed their troubles aren't over.

After re-upholstering the furniture the family are in for a shock, as Blakey pays them an unexpected visit. An emergency bus service has been put in place and he requires Stan's help, but that is not all he ends up getting when he recognises the material on their furniture.

CAST:

Stan	Reg Varney
Mum	Doris Hare
Arthur	Michael Robbins
Olive	Anna Karen
Jack	Bob Grant
The Inspector	Stephen Lewis
The Woman Passenger	Olive Mercer
Joe	Eric Francis

DESIGNER:	Alan Hunter-Craig
PRODUCER:	Stuart Allen

Series 4, Episode 10 – 'Safety First'
Written by Ronald Wolfe and Ronald Chesney
Original Transmission: Sunday 31st January 1971 at 7.25 p.m.

An accident aboard Stan's bus while it is leaving the depot sees the Inspector get into an embarrassing predicament with a female passenger. She is far from happy and reports the incident to the management, leaving Blakey furious at Stan who caused the accident by breaking suddenly, but the hapless Inspector is still left open to ridicule from Jack and Stan.

As a result of the incident the company introduces a new set of signals for the conductor to use to lead the bus out of the depot smoothly and prevent any further accidents. However, things don't go to plan and the whole procedure has to be reviewed. The new system that is put in place requires the buses to exit via the back doors of the depot and enter through the front.

Stan soon errs by bringing his bus into the depot through the back doors and Blakey orders him to turn the bus around. However, while following Jack's directions Stan manages to reverse the bus into the Inspector's office, leaving Blakey trapped in the bars of his door. What will this mean for Stan and the new safety measures? And will hospital-bound Blakey be able to forgive him?

CAST:

Stan	Reg Varney
Mum	Doris Hare
The Inspector	Stephen Lewis
Jack	Bob Grant
Arthur	Michael Robbins
Olive	Anna Karen
The Lady Passenger	Ruth Holden
The Maintenance Man	Michael Slater
The Clippie	Juel Morrell
The Nurse	Gina Warwick
DESIGNER:	Alan Hunter-Craig
PRODUCER:	Stuart Allen

Series 4, Episode 11 – 'The Lodger'
Written by Ronald Wolfe and Ronald Chesney
Original Transmission: Sunday 7th February 1971 at 7.25 p.m.

Decimalisation is crippling the Butlers financially and they consider taking in a lodger. None other than Stan's nemesis, Inspector Blake, informs him that a Transport Manager is coming to the area for a few months and is looking for accommodation. It doesn't take long for the preparations for the new lodger to get under way.

With the imminent arrival of the Transport Manager, Arthur takes it upon himself to rearrange Stan's room. He not only removes his bed and puts it in the lodger's room, replacing it with a camp bed, but he also takes Stan's wardrobe and rug in a bid to furnish the room further. Stan feels as though he is the one that has made all the sacrifices for the lodger, and all without his consent.

The lodger soon starts to rub the Butlers up the wrong way. He commandeers the bathroom, and when he makes a pass at Olive watch out for the fireworks.

CAST:

Stan	Reg Varney
Mum	Doris Hare
Arthur	Michael Robbins
Olive	Anna Karen
The Inspector	Stephen Lewis
Jack	Bob Grant
Mr Nichols	Campbell Singer
Winnie	Winifred Braemar
The Assistant Traffic Manager	Samantha Birch

DESIGNER:	Alan Hunter-Craig
PRODUCER:	Stuart Allen

Series 4, Episode 12 – 'The Injury'
Written by Ronald Wolfe and Ronald Chesney
Original Transmission: Sunday 14th February 1971 at 7.25 p.m.

Stan is redecorating the bathroom, including wallpapering, resiting the shower and fitting new tiles around the bath. Of course Arthur is on hand to criticise the choice of wallpaper and mock Stan when his tiling efforts go awry, but his mood changes from smug to angry when he rips his best trousers after leaning against the glue-coated wall. Not surprisingly, however, he isn't the only one to suffer a mishap. In an attempt to stop the shower from dripping, Stan and Olive fall into the bath, leaving Stan with an injured foot and arm and unfit for work. He faces the prospect of trying to survive for several weeks on sickness benefits.

It is Jack who comes up with an idea to save Stan from this fate. Stan, with great difficulty, makes it to the depot and Jack arranges for him to have an accident there in a bid to earn him some compensation money. A step on a flight of stairs is rigged to collapse and the plan works, but it isn't Stan who is heading for a fall.

CAST:

Stan	Reg Varney
Mum	Doris Hare
Arthur	Michael Robbins
Olive	Anna Karen
Jack	Bob Grant
The Inspector	Stephen Lewis
Joe	Michael Slater
The Nurse	Patricia Shakesby
DESIGNER:	Alan Hunter-Craig
PRODUCER:	Stuart Allen

Series 4, Episode 13 – 'Not Tonight'
Written by Ronald Wolfe and Ronald Chesney
Original Transmission: Sunday 21st February 1971 at 7.25 p.m.

Stan's love life is in crisis, as his supply of girlfriends has dried up. Ridiculed by Inspector Blake and brother-in-law Arthur, his self-esteem and confidence take a blow, but maybe his luck is about to change.

A new employee in the depot's canteen called Stella catches Stan's eye and he moves in quickly to set up a date with her. What he doesn't realise is that she is more interested in his wage packet than in him. However, his spirits are lifted and he takes Stella for a drink accompanied by Jack and his girlfriend, Joyce.

The night proves to be very expensive for Stan, as he spends his wages plying Stella with drinks and cigarettes and she even manages to get him to buy her a new pair of tights. However, when she agrees to pop back to Stan's house for a nightcap he thinks his luck is in, but all he gets from her is a kiss and further expense. Stella then ditches poor, gullible Stan and gives him the cold shoulder at work as she moves on to her next victim, leaving Stan bereft of his wages and humiliated.

CAST:

Stan	Reg Varney
Mum	Doris Hare
Jack	Bob Grant
The Inspector	Stephen Lewis
Arthur	Michael Robbins
Olive	Anna Karen
Stella	Charlotte Howard
Winnie	Winifred Braemar
Molly	Deirdre Costello
Joyce	Ursula Mohan

DESIGNER:	Alan Hunter-Craig
PRODUCER:	Stuart Allen

Series 5, Episode 1 – 'The Nursery'
Written by Ronald Wolfe and Ronald Chesney
Original Transmission: Sunday 19th September 1971 at 7.25 p.m.

The bus depot has opened up a nursery where the clippies can leave their children while they are at work, but the workload is too much for the nurse and she demands assistance. When Stan hears of the job vacancy and suggests to Olive that she should apply for the job. She doesn't feel as though she could do the job and Arthur agrees – that is, until he hears how much she would earn, at which point his attitude suddenly changes. Mum gives Olive some lessons on how to change nappies with the aid of her old toy doll and even Stan gives her tips before she takes on the job.

Olive is only hours into her new job when she runs into trouble. The nurse has gone for her lunch break, leaving Olive to cope on her own, but this becomes impossible when she smashes her spectacles. She needs to go home to retrieve her other pair of glasses, leaving Stan and Jack in charge of the babies on their lunch break. Hunger sees them eating the baby food as they wait for Olive to return, but when Blakey catches them they find themselves in trouble.

CAST:

Stan	Reg Varney
Mum	Doris Hare
Arthur	Michael Robbins
Olive	Anna Karen
Jack	Bob Grant
The Inspector	Stephen Lewis
The Nurse	Ruth Kettlewell
The Clippie	Laura Graham

DESIGNER:	Alan Hunter-Craig
PRODUCER:	Derrick Goodwin

Series 5, Episode 2 – 'Stan's Room'
Written by Ronald Wolfe and Ronald Chesney
Original Transmission: Sunday 26th September 1971 at 7.25 p.m.

Stan brings home a clippie called Doreen and is hoping for a chance to have a kiss and cuddle on the sofa with her, but he is thwarted by his family who are watching a late-night film on the television. He tries his luck on the armchair in the back room, but constant interruptions from Arthur, Olive and mum drive Doreen away.

A fed-up Stan moves out of the Butler house and the only option left open to him is to move into Blakey's spare room. Perhaps he would have been better staying at home, as Blake asks for rent in advance, bans alcohol and female visitors, and won't allow any late nights out.

That night Stan is determined not to be put off by these restrictions and he takes Doreen back to his new home. However, he has to figure out how to get her upstairs without Blakey hearing her footsteps and so resorts to giving her a piggyback. Just when Stan thinks his luck is finally in, his family track him down and pay him a visit, thus ruining his chance of romance with Doreen. His mum pleads with him to return home, but Stan feels that he needs a place of his own. However, she has the last say on the matter.

CAST:

Stan	Reg Varney
Mum	Doris Hare
Arthur	Michael Robbins
Olive	Anna Karen
Jack	Bob Grant
The Inspector	Stephen Lewis
Doreen	Pat Ashton
DESIGNER:	Alan Hunter-Craig
PRODUCER:	Derrick Goodwin

Series 5, Episode 3 – 'The Best Man'
Written by Ronald Wolfe and Ronald Chesney
Original Transmission: Sunday 3rd October 1971 at 7.25 p.m.

Inspector Blake's niece is getting married to a busman and, as if that isn't bad enough for Blakey, Stan is to be the best man at the wedding. When he hears of Stan and Jack's plans for a bachelor party for the bridegroom, Bill, the night before his wedding he pictures them getting drunk and being in no fit state to make it to the church on time.

The inebriated bachelor party attendees stagger into the Butler house in the early hours of the morning. Bill is paralytic and so Stan and Jack take the opportunity to mix up a hangover cure for him using raw eggs. However, all they manage to do is make a mess and awaken a furious Arthur, and even more trouble lies ahead.

Stan has to contend with a massive hangover the following morning and Bill is still the worse for wear. What's more, Stan has yet to rehearse his speech and later finds out that he can't remove the wedding ring, which he had placed on his little finger for safe keeping. This proves to be a very uncomfortable experience for him, but the ring will have to come off if the wedding is to go ahead as planned.

CAST:

Stan	Reg Varney
Mum	Doris Hare
Arthur	Michael Robbins
Olive	Anna Karen
Jack	Bob Grant
The Inspector	Stephen Lewis
The Vicar	Robin Parkinson
Sally	Sandra Miller
Bill	Hugh Walters
DESIGNER:	Alan Hunter-Craig
PRODUCER:	Derrick Goodwin

Series 5, Episode 4 – 'The Inspector's Pets'
Written by Ronald Wolfe and Ronald Chesney
Original Transmission: Sunday 10th October 1971 at 7.30 p.m.

Blakey is all set for a few days' holiday, but he has to cancel it because he can't get anyone to look after his pets. As a result, he's is like a bear with a sore head. When Stan damages his bus by hitting a bollard he fears the wrath of Blakey and realises that he could face severe punishment. His only hope is to make sure that Blakey goes on holiday as planned and so he offers to take care of his pets.

This arrangement is agreed and the Butlers are landed with the Inspector's pet dog and fish for a few days. Arthur takes the dog out for a walk via the pub and Stan is concerned that the pub's Dalmatian dog has had its way with Blakey's pedigree dog, while at home Olive causes the fish tank's power to short. In his desperate attempt to fix the problem, Stan cracks the tank's glass and panic ensues, as water is leaking out and putting the fish in danger. Stan has the job of trying to repair the broken tank before Blakey returns from his holiday, but all is well that ends well.

CAST:

Stan	Reg Varney
Mum	Doris Hare
Arthur	Michael Robbins
Olive	Anna Karen
Jack	Bob Grant
The Inspector	Stephen Lewis
Harry	Don McKillop
The Taxi Driver	Terry Duggan
DESIGNER:	Alan Hunter-Craig
PRODUCER:	Derrick Goodwin

Series 5, Episode 5 – 'The Epidemic'
Written by Ronald Wolfe and Ronald Chesney
Original Transmission: Sunday 17th October 1971 at 9.25 p.m.

An outbreak of flu at the bus depot is good news for Stan and Jack. The company arrange for the entire staff to undergo a medical examination so that the fit can be given a flu jab and the flu-infected can be sent home. Stan and Jack are dubious at first, but when they hear that those deemed fit for work will be guaranteed overtime they are the first in line for their injection.

Stan sees this as an opportunity to earn plenty of overtime pay and doesn't want to risk catching the flu from the rest of the family, so he wants them all to have a flu jab. However, they decline, and in any case it may be too late as Olive is already showing early symptoms of the bug.

In addition to the overtime, another incentive to remain fit is that the boyfriend of a clippie Stan fancies has the flu and so she might have spare time on her hands. A booster jab leaves Stan feeling fine, but at home the whole family have now succumbed to the flu, leaving him to look after them. He is determined to avoid their germs at whatever cost and that means taking extreme precautions - but will it all be in vain?

CAST:

Stan	Reg Varney
Mum	Doris Hare
Arthur	Michael Robbins
Olive	Anna Karen
Jack	Bob Grant
The Inspector	Stephen Lewis
The Nurse	Ruth Kettlewell
Sandra	Sharon Young
Eileen	Cheryl Hall
The Barman	Philip Dunbar
Brian	Keith Norrish

DESIGNER:	Alan Hunter-Craig
PRODUCER:	Derrick Goodwin

Series 5, Episode 6 – 'The Busmen's Ball'
Written by Ronald Wolfe and Ronald Chesney
Original Transmission: Sunday 24th October 1971 at 7.25 p.m.

It is the annual Busmen's Ball at the bus depot and instead of the usual conjuring act Stan and Jack ask Blakey to hire a stripper. He is disgusted and denies their request, but they won't be put off and warn him that the busmen will boycott the event unless a stripper is hired. The Inspector refuses to be blackmailed, but Stan and Jack will not rest until they get their way.

At home Olive is also looking forward to the Busmen's Ball, but Arthur announces that they won't be going as the previous year's event ended in a brawl. Minutes later, however, when Jack pops in to tell Stan that the dance committee for the ball have agreed to having a stripper at the event, Arthur has a sudden change of heart and tells his wife that they will go to the ball after all.

Preparations for the Ball see Olive faced with a dress-making dilemma and she enlists the help of Stan, Arthur and a tailor's dummy to create something to wear to the event. The Busmen's Ball runs anything but smoothly, however, leaving Olive distressed, but Stan is happy in the end.

CAST:

Stan	Reg Varney
Mum	Doris Hare
Arthur	Michael Robbins
Olive	Anna Karen
Jack	Bob Grant
The Inspector	Stephen Lewis
Elsie	Wendy Richard
Chalkie	Glen Whitter
DESIGNER:	Alan Hunter-Craig
PRODUCER:	Derrick Goodwin

Series 5, Episode 7 – 'Canteen Trouble'
Written by Ronald Wolfe and Ronald Chesney
Original Transmission: Sunday 31st October 1971 at 7.25 p.m.

The canteen is running at a loss, but Stan and Jack aren't complaining. As they are friends with the canteen lady she makes sure that they get massive portions for the same price as everyone else. Blakey, on the other hand, gets the rough end of the deal and he begins to suspect that Stan is getting too much for his money. Stan is also receiving free handouts of food, which he takes home to the family. His luck, however, is soon to run out.

Blake sacks Suzy, the unscrupulous canteen employee, and replaces her with Gladys, who is miserly with her helpings and is an ex-prison warden. Jack is convinced that she can be corrupted and turns on the charm with her, leading her to believe that Stan fancies her – and it works. Gladys arranges for Stan to pay her a visit in order to give him some food, but how will she want paying? Stan soon discovers what Gladys wants in return and is not at all keen on the idea, but she will not be denied. Blakey makes a welcome entrance, inadvertently coming to Stan's rescue, but he uncovers his attempts to smuggle food out of the depot. The Inspector comes up with a solution that he is sure will foil any further pilfering from the canteen.

CAST:

Stan	Reg Varney
Mum	Doris Hare
Arthur	Michael Robbins
Olive	Anna Karen
Jack	Bob Grant
The Inspector	Stephen Lewis
Suzy	Andrea Lawrence
Gladys	Fanny Carby
Chalkie	Glen Whitter
Joan	Luan Peters
DESIGNER:	Alan Hunter-Craig
PRODUCER:	Derrick Goodwin

Series 5, Episode 8 – 'The New Nurse'
Written by Ronald Wolfe and Ronald Chesney
Original Transmission: Sunday 7th November 1971 at 7.25 p.m.

The Butlers are going through another financial crisis and are forced to take in another lodger. When Mary, the new bus depot nurse, overhears that Stan has a spare room she declares an interest and after viewing the room agrees to move in. Her upper-class attitude appeals to Arthur and he immediately takes a shine to her, much to the displeasure of Olive.

It is clear that trouble is around the corner, with Arthur pandering to Mary's every need while Stan isn't impressed and feels that the new lodger is a snob. When wisecracks are made at his expense Arthur distances himself from the family and starts making advances towards Mary. He resorts to having a bath, changing into a suit and shaving before sitting down to dinner in a bid to impress.

Things threaten to get out of control when Arthur and Olive argue and he ends up taking Mary to the cinema instead of his wife. As it turns out, however, Olive has the last laugh when Arthur has to rethink his recent behaviour and grovel to his wife for forgiveness after he is spurned by Mary.

CAST:

Stan	Reg Varney
Mum	Doris Hare
Arthur	Michael Robbins
Olive	Anna Karen
Jack	Bob Grant
Inspector	Stephen Lewis
Mary	Hal Dyer
Sally	Sandra Miller
George	Keith Norrish
DESIGNER:	Alan Hunter-Craig
PRODUCER:	Derrick Goodwin

Series 5, Episode 9 – 'Lost Property'
Written by Ronald Wolfe and Ronald Chesney
Original Transmission: Sunday 14th November 1971 at 7.25 p.m.

Stan and Jack find some fish and chips on their bus and help themselves, but when a passenger reports the loss to Blakey trouble ensues. Remains of the fish are found by the cleaners and Blakey promises changes in regard to lost property. He warns the busmen that at the end of every journey the bus will be checked for lost property and a form completed.

The new rules don't go down well with the bus crews and they unite to wind Inspector Blake up, with Stan and Jack taking on mock lost property en route. On their return to the depot it is up to Blakey to list a number of embarrassing items as lost property prior to discovering that he has been the victim of a practical joke.

It is no laughing matter for Stan, however, when he takes home an envelope found on his bus instead of handing it in to lost property. The envelope, which contains a diamond, ends up getting ripped and a full-scale search of Arthur and Olive's bed is needed. If the diamond can't be found Stan faces the real possibility of the sack.

CAST:

Stan	Reg Varney
Mum	Doris Hare
Arthur	Michael Robbins
Olive	Anna Karen
Jack	Bob Grant
Inspector	Stephen Lewis
Woman	Amelia Bayntun
Joe	Bartlett Mullins

DESIGNER:	Alan Hunter-Craig
PRODUCER:	Derrick Goodwin

Series 5, Episode 10 – 'Stan's Uniform'
Written by Ronald Wolfe and Ronald Chesney
Original Transmission: Sunday 21st November 1971 at 7.25 p.m.

Stan comes home from work to find that the drain requires unblocking, but he sees no need to change out of his uniform. It is a decision that he will live to regret. Olive pours a basinful of mucky water containing tea leaves down the drain, covering Stan and his uniform. He doesn't see any cause for panic though, as he is confident that the bus company will put it down to wear and tear and replace it free of charge.

However, Inspector Blake has other ideas and tells Stan that he will have to wait six months for a new uniform. Stan is gobsmacked. Jack comes up with a plan, involving Stan taking his uniform to the dry cleaners and it ending up in tatters. It is a plot that works, as Blakey is forced to relent and issue him with a new uniform.

When Stan goes home to show his new uniform to the family a disaster awaits. He sits down to have a cup of tea, unaware that Arthur has just painted the chair. Coated in paint, Stan's new jacket and trousers need urgent attention and he heads down to the maintenance department at the depot for assistance in removing the paint. Stan and Jack have to use their initiative but only succeed in ruining the new uniform, leaving Stan with an expensive bill for a replacement unless he can find another solution.

CAST:

Stan	Reg Varney
Mum	Doris Hare
Arthur	Michael Robbins
Olive	Anna Karen
Jack	Bob Grant
Inspector	Stephen Lewis
Nobby	Norman Mitchell
George	Brian Grellis
DESIGNER:	Alan Hunter-Craig
PRODUCER:	Derrick Goodwin

Series 5, Episode 11 – 'The Strain'
Written by Ronald Wolfe and Ronald Chesney
Original Transmission: Sunday 28th November 1971 at 7.25 p.m.

Stan gets involved in a silly prank in the canteen. When trying to guess the weight of his girlfriend he is asked to lift her up and in doing so he injures his back. This means that he has to miss the rest of his shift and go home to wait for his doctor's prognosis.

The doctor prescribes tablets and rest for Stan and warns him against working for two weeks, but Stan is adamant that he must get back to work as soon as possible. Much to Arthur's amusement, the only solution is for Stan to wear a corset to protect his back from any further strain.

A very stiff Stan returns to work, although he is still in a great deal of discomfort especially with the corset on, and he has to hope that Blakey doesn't sign him off as unfit. Another reason for Stan to be at work is that he has a date arranged with Doreen, his girlfriend. When he brings Doreen home his corset has to come off, causing much hilarity on her part. He soon discovers that without the corset his immobility comes back to haunt him and this ends up ruining his night.

CAST:

Stan	Reg Varney
Mum	Doris Hare
Arthur	Michael Robbins
Olivc	Anna Karen
Jack	Bob Grant
Inspector	Stephen Lewis
Doreen	Pat Ashton
Dr Clark	James Bree
Vic	Nosher Powell
Busman	Keith Norrish

DESIGNER:	Alan Hunter-Craig
PRODUCER:	Derrick Goodwin

Series 5, Episode 12 – 'The New Telly'
Written by Ronald Wolfe and Ronald Chesney
Original Transmission: Sunday 5th December 1971 at 7.25 p.m.

Stan has received his Christmas Club money at the bus depot and has his heart set on buying a colour television. However, unless the Butlers can sell their old black and white set they will not be able to afford one, as Arthur refuses to put any money towards the new television. The problem is finding someone gullible enough to buy their old TV.

When Jack pays the Butlers a visit he tries to improve the situation by adjusting the settings on their TV. It may be a quick and temporary fix, but it will do, and they plan to try to sell the set to their nemesis Blakey, who just happens to be in the market for a TV and also has Christmas Club money to spend.

Before buying the TV Blakey wants to see it working and it would appear that Jack's adjustments have worked when he agrees to buy it. Things aren't that simple though, and after a number of hours in use the TV set blows up, leaving Blakey injured and confined to bed. As a result he threatens to sue Stan and so, in an attempt to appease Blakey, Stan uses his Christmas Club money to buy him a new TV and the whole family pay him a visit. However, the last thing he needs when convalescing is to have the Butlers, Rudges and Jack adding to his misery.

CAST:

Stan	Reg Varney
Mum	Doris Hare
Arthur	Michael Robbins
Olive	Anna Karen
Jack	Bob Grant
The Inspector	Stephen Lewis
Eileen	Shirley Steedman
George	David Richardson
Busman	Keith Norrish
TV Commentator	Peter Cockburn
DESIGNER:	Alan Hunter-Craig
PRODUCER:	Derrick Goodwin

Series 5, Episode 13 – 'Vacancy For Inspector'

Written by Bob Grant and Stephen Lewis
Original Transmission: Sunday 12th December 1971 at 7.25 p.m.

When a vacancy for Inspector comes up at the bus depot Blakey sees it as an opportunity to end the problems caused by Stan and Jack. He promotes Jack to Inspector, much to Stan's displeasure, but Jack promises him favours once he takes up his new post, such as all the overtime and the first pick of the clippies on his bus. However, Stan is in for a nasty shock.

Once Jack has become Inspector he goes through a total personality change and all of his promises to Stan are forgotten. He berates his old friend for his untidiness and worse is sure to follow, as Blakey asks Jack to help him get rid of Stan once and for all. A reluctant Jack agrees to help him, as he is warned that his post is not yet assured.

Blakey is holding all the cards and he learns of all Stan's tricks, including being clocked in for duty illegally and stealing from the canteen, and so Stan is put in his place. However, Jack does feel bad about getting his friend into trouble and takes the decision to resign from his new post and return to being Stan's friend and layabout conductor.

CAST:

Stan	Reg Varney
Mum	Doris Hare
Arthur	Michael Robbins
Olive	Anna Karen
Jack	Bob Grant
The Inspector	Stephen Lewis
Christine	Madeleine Mills
Chalkie	Glen Whitter

DESIGNER:	Alan Hunter-Craig
PRODUCER:	Derrick Goodwin

Series 5, Episode 14 – 'A Thin Time'
Written by Bob Grant and Stephen Lewis
Original Transmission: Sunday 19th December 1971 at 7.25 p.m.

Arthur is attracted to a clippie but has a problem. She has a soft spot for men with a full head of hair and a liking of physical fitness. He goes to great lengths to meet those requirements and is prepared to go to great expense too, despite the family's precarious financial position.

While Stan is begging Blakey for overtime to help pay the bills and even taking on cleaning duties to earn more money, Arthur is investing his savings in a collection of expensive wigs in a bid to impress the clippie called Beryl.

When his secret is found out he has to take merciless leg pulling from Stan, but will it be worthwhile and what will Olive's reaction be? Olive and mum are disgusted, and although Arthur promises not to keep the wigs he is determined to try to impress Beryl. His efforts are all in vain, however, as an accident on Stan's bus sees him lose his wig and reveal his baldness to Beryl. All hopes of romance for Arthur end, but Olive is always there for him.

CAST:

Stan	Reg Varney
Mum	Doris Hare
Arthur	Michael Robbins
Olive	Anna Karen
Jack	Bob Grant
The Inspector	Stephen Lewis
Beryl	Alex Marshall
DESIGNER:	Alan Hunter-Craig
PRODUCER:	Derrick Goodwin

Series 5, Episode 15 – 'Boxing Day Social'
Written by Ronald Wolfe and Ronald Chesney
Original Transmission: Sunday 26th December 1971 at 7.25 p.m.

Arthur's mother and sister come to stay with the Butlers over the festive period. Jack takes a fancy to Arthur's sister, Linda, and wants to take her to the forthcoming annual Boxing Day Social event at the depot, but Arthur insists that she is above such things. However, Linda has other ideas and is looking forward to attending.

The Butler and Rudge families descend on the bus depot for the festivities with mixed feelings, and emotions soon begin to run high. Jack is getting a little too familiar with Linda for her brother's liking and Olive adds to his problems by getting drunk. She takes offence at Arthur's philandering and proceeds to make an exhibition of herself and a full-scale argument breaks out between the Butlers and Rudges.

If that wasn't bad enough, a fight almost ensues when Arthur warns Jack to stay away from his sister, much to her disappointment, and the fireworks don't end there. Linda wants to have a look at one of the buses and Stan gives her a tour, but she uses the chance to try to seduce him. This spells trouble, as he is caught in the act, and ensures that the night ends on a low for poor Stan.

CAST:

Stan	Reg Varney
Mum	Doris Hare
Arthur	Michael Robbins
Olive	Anna Karen
Jack	Bob Grant
The Inspector	Stephen Lewis
Mrs Rudge	Gillian Lind
Linda	Helen Fraser
Beryl	Janice Hoy
Busman	Kenneth Waller
DESIGNER:	Alan Hunter-Craig
PRODUCER:	Derrick Goodwin

Series 6, Episode 1 – 'No Smoke Without Fire'
Written by Bob Grant and Stephen Lewis
Original Transmission: Sunday 20th February 1972 at 7.25 p.m.

After a fire at the bus depot Inspector Blake bans smoking in the workplace and also aboard the buses. Jack is adamant that Stan won't be able to stop smoking and when he disagrees the pair place a bet on it.

It proves a difficult task for Stan, who takes to eating sweets to beat the craving for a cigarette while his appetite also increases. When he arrives home he extends his bet to Arthur, who is certain that he could quit smoking without any problems. However, Arthur is intent on cheating and hides his cigarettes strategically. In the end, both find the craving too strong and are caught by each other breaking the ban.

At work, when their bus breaks down, Stan and Jack use the opportunity to have some fun with a pair of trainee clippies, but they are interrupted when Blakey arrives on the scene aboard a following bus. Stan is almost caught having a sly cigarette, but he manages to discard it in the used-ticket bin. This is to spell disaster.

Blakey orders Stan to take the bus back to the depot and stays aboard to make sure that there are no more delays, and everyone is totally oblivious to the fact that the discarded cigarette is still burning. Within minutes the bus is ablaze. Blakey is trapped upstairs and life is in the hands of Stan and Jack, who face the task of rescuing him.

CAST:

Stan	Reg Varney
Mum	Doris Hare
Arthur	Michael Robbins
Olive	Anna Karen
Jack	Bob Grant
The Inspector	Stephen Lewis
Frieda	Pauline Cunningham
Suzy	Mary Land
Gladys	Eunice Black
DESIGNER:	Alan Hunter-Craig
PRODUCER:	Derrick Goodwin

Series 6, Episode 2 – 'Love Is What You Make It'
Written by George Layton and Jonathan Lynn
Original Transmission: Sunday 27th February 1972 at 7.25 p.m.

Arthur and Olive's arguments are getting out of hand and Stan is fed up with them. He suggests that they go to see a marriage guidance counsellor in a bid to sort out their problems, but Arthur refuses. Undeterred, Stan takes Olive and his mum to see the counsellor, who suggests that she makes an effort to make herself more desirable to her husband.

When Arthur returns from work he is in for a shock, as Olive has undergone a makeover and has prepared a candlelit dinner. However, his reaction is not what she was hoping for. She receives insults instead of compliments and is reduced to tears before he rushes out to the pub.

Stan has another plan lined up. He intends to make Arthur jealous by having him find Olive with another man. There is just one snag: who would be stupid enough to do it? Jack knows just the man for the job and gets Inspector Blake to visit the Butler house under false pretences. The plan goes a little awry, however, when Olive doesn't follow the script. Arthur comes home to find his wife and the Inspector on the floor together, but what will his reaction be?

CAST:

Stan	Reg Varney
Mum	Doris Hare
Arthur	Michael Robbins
Olive	Anna Karen
Jack	Bob Grant
The Inspector	Stephen Lewis
Clippie in Canteen	Jacqui Cook
Marriage Counsellor	Aubrey Morris
Window Cleaner	Johnny Briggs

DESIGNER:	Alan Hunter-Craig
PRODUCER:	Bryan Izzard

Series 6, Episode 3 – 'Private Hire'
Written by Bob Grant and Stephen Lewis
Original Transmission: Sunday 5th March 1972 at 7.25 p.m.

Stan is in a precarious financial position. He has blown all of his wages betting on Jack's racing tips and has yet to hand over his housekeeping money. In desperation, Stan borrows money from a workmate but is threatened with violence if he doesn't get his money back on time.

Jack comes up with an idea to make some money when an employee reveals that she needs help with moving house. Under the pretence that they are taking a bus out on tests at Blakey's request, Stan and Jack use the bus as a removal van and charge for their services.

The bus is packed to capacity with furniture when they are caught in the act by a suspicious Blakey. While Jack drags Stan into the bookmakers to gamble away the money they have just earned he drives their bus back to the depot, leaving them in hot water.

Stan is still short of money and so Jack encourages him to indulge in more dodgy dealings. The idea is to borrow a coach for an old-age pensioner's trip, which could see them earning a nice sum of money. The snag is that they don't have permission to use the coach and Blakey is waiting to foil their plan, but what will it cost Stan?

CAST:

Stan	Reg Varney
Mum	Doris Hare
Arthur	Michael Robbins
Olive	Anna Karen
Jack	Bob Grant
The Inspector	Stephen Lewis
Basher	Maurice Bush
Iris	Ursula Mohan
Iris's Mum	Mary Maxted
Chalkie	Glen Whitter

DESIGNER:	Alan Hunter-Craig
PRODUCER:	Bryan Izzard

Series 6, Episode 4 – 'Stan's Worst Day'
Written by Bob Grant and Stephen Lewis
Original Transmission: Sunday 12th March 1972 at 7.25 p.m.

Stan finds himself stuck in the middle as Arthur and Olive's marital problems and arguments continue. He also has troubles of his own at work after accidents that see him damage a bus and then proceed to ruin Blakey's new uniform.

It is certainly a disastrous day for Stan and it leads to his reminiscing about the time when he was a conductor and his driver – who was Blakey – had damaged a bus. Back then, Jack had just started work at the depot as a trainee conductor and was in need of somewhere to stay. Stan had suggested he take a look at the spare room at his house, but he had competition. In the end, a hospital porter called Arthur Rudge (with a full head of hair) beats Jack to the room but had to contend with Mrs Butler's attempts to matchmake him with her daughter, Olive. When a drunken Arthur mistakenly got into bed with Olive it turned out to be a terrible mistake, as Mrs Butler insisted he'd have to marry her daughter.

Reminiscing aside, Arthur and Olive come to a decision. They believe that Stan is the cause of their arguments and that he should move out. Stan is left gobsmacked.

CAST:

Stan	Reg Varney
Mum	Doris Hare
Arthur	Michael Robbins
Olive	Anna Karen
Jack	Bob Grant
The Inspector	Stephen Lewis
The Painter	Terry Duggan
The Mechanic	John M. East
The Manager	Frederick Hall

DESIGNER:	Alan Hunter-Craig
PRODUCER:	Derrick Goodwin

Series 6, Episode 5 – 'Union Trouble'
Written by Bob Grant and Stephen Lewis
Original Transmission: Sunday 19th March 1972 at 7.25 p.m.

When Elsie, the canteen employee, is sacked by Blakey following alterations to the canteen's opening hours Stan is outraged and Shop Steward Jack calls everyone out on strike. However, before the planned walkout is under way, Blakey arranges for Jack to receive a productivity bonus payment, thus persuading him to call off the strike. But Stan has other ideas and refuses to return to work until Elsie is reinstated. The problem is that his strike is unofficial and not supported by the union, which means he won't receive any strike pay.

Stan's fight goes on and he stages a protest by refusing to get out of his driver's cab, causing disruption. Blakey is intent on getting him out of the cab, denying him food, physically trying to drag him out of the cab and luring him out with a cup of tea. It is Blakey's guile that wins out, but Stan is adamant that his strike will go on.

Once Stan finds that he is working harder at home than he does at work, however, he decides to call off his strike and return to work. Blakey wants Stan to suffer for his actions and suspends him without pay, but someone comes to Stan's rescue.

CAST:

Stan	Reg Varney
Mum	Doris Hare
Arthur	Michael Robbins
Olive	Anna Karen
Jack	Bob Grant
The Inspector	Stephen Lewis
Elsie	Marcia Ashton
Chalkie	Glen Whitter

DESIGNER:	Alan Hunter-Craig
PRODUCER:	Bryan Izzard

Series 6, Episode 6 – 'Bye Bye Blakey'
Written by George Layton and Jonathan Lynn
Original Transmission: Sunday 26th March 1972 at 7.25 p.m.

The employees are to have their medicals at the bus depot and that includes Inspector Blake, much to his discomfort. For Stan and Jack it's a chance to ridicule him, but they are alarmed when they overhear the doctor and Blakey talking about the fact that he won't be around much longer and assume that their nemesis is soon to die.

Stan and Jack start to feel guilty about the way they have treated Blakey over the years and go out of their way to make what they believe to be his last few days bearable. They even vow to take their bus out on time and Stan invites Blakey around to his house for tea.

At the depot the employees decide to have a collection to buy Inspector Blake a present, and it is only after he receives his gift that the confusion is cleared up. It is revealed that Blakey is not about to die but is set to leave the depot for another job. Suddenly Stan and Jack's attitudes towards him revert to type.

CAST:

Stan	Reg Varney
Mum	Doris Hare
Arthur	Michael Robbins
Olive	Anna Karen
Jack	Bob Grant
The Inspector	Stephen Lewis
Mr Stilton	Garfield Morgan
The Clippie	Petra Siniawski
The Nurse	Catherine Kessler
The Lady Doctor	Nicolette Roeg
The Bus Driver	Philip Dunbar

DESIGNER:	Alan Hunter-Craig
PRODUCER:	Derrick Goodwin

Series 6, Episode 7 – 'The Prize'
Written by George Layton and Jonathan Lynn
Original Transmission: Sunday 2nd April 1972 at 7.25 p.m.

A raffle run by Inspector Blake sees mum win a holiday for two in the Costa Brava. This poses a difficult question: whom will she take with her? Each member of the family believes that they have valid reasons to be chosen for the Costa Brava trip and they set out to win mum over.

Mum finds that she doesn't have to worry about doing any housework, as the family are going out of their way to impress her. Stan and Arthur both make her breakfast and they also buy her flowers, while Olive helps her with the shopping. Competition for the right to holiday with mum is getting very serious.

Someone, however, is in for a disappointment when Inspector Blake pays Mrs Butler a visit. Who is destined for the sun? All will soon be revealed.

CAST:

Stan	Reg Varney
Mum	Doris Hare
Arthur	Michael Robbins
Olive	Anna Karen
Jack	Bob Grant
The Inspector	Stephen Lewis
Canteen Girl	Julia Breck

DESIGNER:	Alan Hunter-Craig
PRODUCER:	Bryan Izzard

Series 7, Episode 1 – 'Olive's Divorce'
Written by Ronald Wolfe and Ronald Chesney
Original Transmission: Monday 26th February 1973 at 8.30 p.m.

The Rudge marriage has finally broken up and Arthur has moved out of the Butler house. It is a very emotional time for Olive, who has to go through the ordeal of appearing in the divorce court, so she needs all the support she can get from her mum and brother Stan.

After a stressful day in court, Stan is looking forward to a night out at the pictures with a clippie called Sandra. However, he cannot leave Olive at home alone and is forced to take her with him on his date.

Stan's hopes for any romantic encounters at the cinema are thwarted, as his sister keeps interrupting his attempted amorous advances towards Sandra. However, it seems the night still holds promise when his date invites him back to her place, and he thinks his luck is in when he manages to con Blakey into escorting Olive home. He is in for a surprise though. Will it ruin his romantic intentions once again?

CAST:

Stan	Reg Varney
Inspector	Stephen Lewis
Mum	Doris Hare
Jack	Bob Grant
Olive	Anna Karen
Sandra	Sandra Bryant
DESIGNERS:	Rodney Cammish and Alan Hunter-Craig
PRODUCER:	Bryan Izzard

Series 7, Episode 2 – 'The Perfect Clippie'
Written by George Layton and Jonathan Lynn
Original Transmission: Sunday 4th March 1973 at 8.30 p.m.

Although Olive is still reeling from her divorce, the lack of finances coming into the household forces Stan to give Olive an ultimatum: either find another man to keep her or seek a job.

In a bid to help, Stan grovels to Blakey and manages to get Olive a job as a clippie at the depot. The Inspector gives Jack the task of training her aboard Stan's bus and it proves to be a very testing shift for Stan and Jack.

Olive quickly tests their patience when she takes every opportunity to quote from the rule book. Throughout her first shift she recites regulations, rebuking Jack for failing to do his job properly. Stan isn't exempt from criticism either and soon it all becomes a bit too much to bear.

Blakey is impressed by Olive's efficiency and also gleeful when she reveals Stan and Jack's failings on duty. They, on the other hand, are furious and realise that something must be done to stop Blakey and Olive's obsession with the rule book, so they hatch a plan.

CAST:

Stan	Reg Varney
Mum	Doris Hare
Olive	Anna Karen
Inspector	Stephen Lewis
Jack	Bob Grant
Doctor	Frederick Peisley
Tough Passenger	Peter Davidson

FILM SEQUENCES:	
CAMERA:	Barry Noakes
SOUND:	Alan Mills and Malcolm Bristow
EDITOR:	Eddy Lowe
DESIGNERS:	Rodney Cammish and Alan Hunter-Craig
PRODUCER:	Bryan Izzard

Series 7, Episode 3 – 'The Ticket Machine'
Written by Bob Grant and Stephen Lewis
Original Transmission: Sunday 11th March 1973 at 8.30 p.m.

When Olive and mum become mail-order agents it is a recipe for disaster. They order goods from a catalogue without reading the terms of the agreement with the mail-order firm and Stan points out that they have made a huge mistake. Things get even worse when a tea set gets smashed and Olive rips a dress and then sits on a guitar, leaving them in debt with no hope of selling the goods.

Jack comes up with a plan to earn some extra money to dig Stan out of trouble. The plan involves his acquiring a stolen ticket machine, which Jack will then use to sell tickets without Blakey knowing. Although Stan hates the idea he realises that he has no other option if he is to make enough money to pay off the family's debts.

The plan is fraught with danger from the start, as the police arrive at the depot to investigate the theft of the ticket machine. Blakey is keen to catch the culprit and cannot believe his luck when he pays the Butlers a visit and finds a discarded ticket from the stolen machine. This spells trouble for Stan, but will it cost him money or his job?

CAST:

Stan	Reg Varney
Jack	Bob Grant
Mum	Doris Hare
Olive	Anna Karen
Inspector	Stephen Lewis
Manager	Michael Sheard

DESIGNER:	Rodney Cammish
PRODUCER:	Bryan Izzard

Series 7, Episode 4 – 'The Poster'
Written by Wally Malstan and Garry Chambers
Original Transmission: Sunday 18th March 1973 at 8.30 p.m.

The Luxton and District Traction Company are looking to recruit new staff and are keen to improve their public image and boost passenger numbers. It is announced that one driver will be chosen to appear on a recruitment poster and they will receive a bonus payment.

Jack sees this as an opportunity to earn a share of the payment and promises Stan that his job will be safeguarded if he wins the right to appear on the poster. Stan is elected to represent the depot, but Blakey is keen to dampen his spirits and informs him of the competition. Other depots are supplying a part-time male model, a footballer-cum-bus driver and a body builder.

In an attempt to spruce up his appearance, Stan is given a makeover with the aid of cosmetics, but he isn't happy with either the results or the consequent leg pulling from his workmates. He therefore decides to use a different ploy and appears in front of the competition panel as his normal scruffy self. His down-to-earth attitude and appearance win the day and the contest, but how long will the poster be in use?

CAST:

Stan	Reg Varney
Jack	Bob Grant
Olive	Anna Karen
Inspector	Stephen Lewis
Mum	Doris Hare
Chemist	Kenneth Gilbert
Chemist's Assistant	Elaine Wells
1st Judge	Michael Sheard
2nd Judge	John Crocker
Finalists	Nicholas Hobbs
	Perry Soblosky
	Folker Henrix

STORIES EDITED BY:	Ronald Wolfe and Ronald Chesney
DESIGNERS:	Rodney Cammish and Alan Hunter-Craig
PRODUCER:	Bryan Izzard

Series 7, Episode 5 – 'The Football Match'

Written by Bob Grant and Stephen Lewis

Original Transmission: Sunday 25th March 1973 at 8.30 p.m.

The bus depot forms its own football team, appointing Inspector Blake as their manager. Stan and Jack show no interest until it is announced that there will be a bonus payment to each player if they win their upcoming game. Blakey warns them that they must train in their own time after work if they want to play in the match.

During their first training session at the depot disaster strikes the team. Their star player, Bob, injures his ankle in an accidental collision with Stan, ruling him out of the match. One man down, it looks certain that the team will be deprived of their potential bonuses - unless Stan can find a replacement.

Stan's search for another player proves fruitless and, in desperation, they are forced to ask Olive to step in. And that isn't the only surprise on match day. Their opponents, The Basildon Bashers, turn out to be a ladies team. With a short-sighted Olive and Jack's greater interest in chatting up the opposition rather than focusing on playing the game, the Luxton side face an uphill battle.

CAST:

Stan	Reg Varney
Jack	Bob Grant
Inspector	Stephen Lewis
Olive	Anna Karen
Mum	Doris Hare
Chalkie	Jules Walter
Bob	Bob McNab
Canteen Girl	Melanie Jane
Eunice	Carol Gillies
Iris	Jennifer Guy
Rita	Jeanette Wild
Mary	Maxine Casson

STORIES EDITED BY:	Ronald Wolfe and Ronald Chesney
FILM SEQUENCES:	
CAMERAS:	Barry Noakes
SOUND:	Alan Mills and Malcolm Bristow
EDITOR:	Eddy Lowe
DESIGNER:	Alan Hunter-Craig
PRODUCER:	Bryan Izzard

Series 7, Episode 6 – 'On The Omnibuses'
Written by Bob Grant and Stephen Lewis
Original Transmission: Sunday 1st April 1973 at 8.30 p.m.

It is the 50th anniversary of the first motor-powered bus at Luxton and District Traction Company and to celebrate there is an exhibition with a number of old buses on display. Stan is in attendance with Olive and mum, but he is exhausted and falls asleep aboard one of the old buses. He begins to dream of life working On The Buses fifty years earlier.

His dream portrays the early days at Luxton and District as not much different from his current reality. Stan's horse-drawn bus crashes into a shop window and he dreads telling Inspector Blake, but Jack tells Stan about the newly formed union that will help him. However, Blakey vows that they will be worked even harder to pay for the damage they have done.

The new motor-powered bus is to be driven by Stan, which leads to Jack's attempts to instigate a strike, but to no avail. On their first trip aboard the new bus mayhem ensues, with mum and Olive involved in the capers, and to cap it all off Stan crashes the new bus. Thankfully it is all just a dream.

CAST:

Stan	Reg Varney
Mum	Doris Hare
Olive	Anna Karen
Inspector	Stephen Lewis
Jack	Bob Grant
Old Lady	Lucy Griffiths
Manager	Paul Dawkins
STORIES EDITED BY:	Ronald Wolfe and Ronald Chesney
FILM SEQUENCES:	
CAMERAS:	Barry Noakes
SOUND:	Alan Mills and Malcolm Bristow
EDITOR:	Eddy Lowe

DESIGNER:	Alan Hunter-Craig
PRODUCER:	Bryan Izzard

Series 7, Episode 7 – 'Goodbye Stan'
Written by Ronald Wolfe and Ronald Chesney
Original Transmission: Sunday 8th April 1973 at 8.30 p.m.

The cost of living is rising, unlike Stan's wages, and he has had enough of his constant financial struggles. Blakey is unsympathetic and refuses his appeals for more overtime, but there is hope for him elsewhere as he has applied for a new job with better wages working in a car factory.

A letter confirming that he has got the job leaves him feeling over the moon, but his family are troubled as the job is in the Midlands, meaning that he will have to leave home. Upset but in preparation for her son's departure mum decides to take in a lodger.

Jack offers Stan the chance of one last scam, suggesting that instead of handing in his notice he should get himself sacked and thus get more money in lieu of notice. Stan sets about winding up Blakey and gets the sack, much to his delight, but Stan has the last laugh and tells his nemesis that he had planned to leave anyway.

Stan has one last drink with his workmates and then bids a tearful farewell to his family as he heads for the Midlands. Stan's room is vacant but is soon to be filled by none other than Inspector Blake.

CAST:

Stan	Reg Varney
Olive	Anna Karen
Jack	Bob Grant
Inspector	Stephen Lewis
Mum	Doris Hare
Chalkie	Jules Walter
Bill	John Lyons

SERIES CREATED AND STORIES EDITED BY:	Ronald Wolfe and Ronald Chesney
DESIGNER:	Rodney Cammish
PRODUCER:	Bryan Izzard

Series 7, Episode 8 – 'Hot Water'
Written by Bob Grant and Stephen Lewis
Original Transmission: Sunday 15th April 1973 at 8.30 a.m.

Inspector Blake is now residing at the Butler house and it doesn't take him long to cause problems. He manages to break the immersion heater and Mrs Butler points out that he will have to pay for repairs and they won't come cheap.

Blakey's domestic troubles see him arrive at work late and unshaven, for which he receives a public tongue-lashing from the manager. Jack may have a solution to his immersion problem and persuades him to part with a small sum of money in return for an immersion heater. Unknown to the Inspector it has been stolen from the canteen, but he has no choice but to accept it as the manager is close to catching him with it on his person.

Fitting the immersion heater is the next problem for Blakey and with Jack's help things go awry. The immersion element doesn't fit and the water tank hasn't been fully drained, and soon the Butler house is awash with water. Can Blakey solve the problem and restore hot water to the Butler household or will Jack have a planned night of romance at his house ruined by unwanted visitors in need of hot water? Time will tell.

CAST:	
Inspector	Stephen Lewis
Olive	Anna Karen
Mum	Doris Hare
Jack	Bob Grant
Joyce	Melanie Jane
Manager	Michael Sheard
STORIES EDITED BY:	Ronald Wolfe and Ronald Chesney
FILM SEQUENCES:	
CAMERAS	Grenville Middleton
SOUND	Derek Rye
EDITOR	Eddy Lowe
DESIGNER:	Alan Hunter-Craig
PRODUCER:	Bryan Izzard

Series 7, Episode 9 – 'The Visit'
Written by George Layton and Jonathan Lynn
Original Transmission: Sunday 22nd April 1973 at 7.25 p.m.

The Butler household is to get a visitor who is sure to cause problems. Blakey's mum pays a visit to Luxton and makes herself at home when the Butlers agree to let her stay for a couple of nights.

On arrival she immediately begins to manipulate and dictate to the Butlers. She also complains about the accommodation and treats Mrs Butler like a servant as she quickly ruffles feathers. Even her son can't avoid her ordering him around and posing embarrassing questions.

Mrs Butler is soon at the end of her tether and things come to a head with a night out at the bingo. When Mrs Blake wins the jackpot on a card paid for by Mrs Butler she refuses to share her winnings and a full-scale argument breaks out. She may not receive a share of the winnings but Mrs Butler does manage to rid herself of the troublesome Mrs Blake.

CAST:

Olive	Anna Karen
Mum	Doris Hare
Inspector	Stephen Lewis
Jack	Bob Grant
Mrs Blake	Pat Nye

SERIES CREATED AND STORIES EDITED BY:	Ronald Wolfe and Ronald Chesney
DESIGNER:	Rodney Cammish
PRODUCER:	Bryan Izzard

Series 7, Episode 10 – 'What The Stars Foretell'
Written by Bob Grant and Stephen Lewis
Original Transmission: Sunday 29th April 1973 at 7.25 p.m.

Horoscopes and tea leaves are telling Olive and her mum that they are both to be married. This spells trouble for Inspector Blake, as they set their sights on him as their potential husband-to-be, much to his horror.

Olive and Mrs Butler are soon in direct competition as they try to win the hand of their hapless lodger, who is adamant that he has no intentions of getting married. Olive attempts to get closer to Blakey in his office and he gets caught in a compromising position with her by the manager, who issues him with a harsh warning.

There is no escape for Blakey on his return home, as Mrs Butler has transformed herself with a makeover and starts making advances. She intends to send Olive off to bingo so that they can spend a romantic evening alone, but her daughter has other ideas. Mother and daughter argue over their rights to Blakey's affections and this leads to chaos, his newspaper getting ripped and his slippers burned in the process.

When it seems as though he may be forced into a marriage he doesn't want, perhaps the horoscopes can come to his rescue?

CAST:

Jack	Bob Grant
Olive	Anna Karen
Inspector	Stephen Lewis
Mum	Doris Hare
Fred	Larry Martyn
Sandra	Sandra Bryant
Wendy	Nina West
Manager	Michael Sheard
STORIES EDITED BY:	Ronald Wolfe and Ronald Chesney
DESIGNER:	Alan Hunter-Craig
PRODUCER:	Bryan Izzard

Series 7, Episode 11 – 'The Allowance'
Written by Miles Rudge
Original Transmission: Sunday 6th May 1973 at 7.25 p.m.

A new clippie at the depot called Jessie is sure to cause problems for Inspector Blake. She is intent on making sure that the clippies get an allowance for having to pay to use public conveniences while on duty. Shop Steward Jack warms to the idea and sees it as another opportunity to cause more problems for Blakey.

The Inspector is against the suggestion of an allowance until Jack backs Jessie up and threatens strike action. Blakey is boxed into a corner and takes the idea to the manager, who feels it would be justified and leaves him to organise it.

After sifting through piles of allowance claims, many of which he believes to be false, he pleads with the manager to cancel the allowance payments. The manager is of the opinion that false claims should be detected by the Inspector and so he sets about checking up on the clippies. However, Jessie is determined to outsmart him.

The whole affair turns into a huge embarrassment for Inspector Blake. Loitering outside public toilets lands him in trouble, so what will become of the allowance payments?

CAST:

Jack	Bob Grant
Olive	Anna Karen
Inspector	Stephen Lewis
Mum	Doris Hare
Jessie	Yootha Joyce
Manager	Michael Sheard
Mrs Webb	Claire Davenport
Sandra	Sandra Bryant
Sid	John Lyons

FILM SEQUENCES:

CAMERAS	Barry Noakes
SOUND	Alan Mills

EDITOR	Ray Weedon
STORIES EDITED BY:	Ronald Wolfe and Ronald Chesney
DESIGNER:	Rodney Cammish
PRODUCER:	Bryan Izzard

Series 7, Episode 12 – 'Friends In High Places'
Written by George Layton and Jonathan Lynn
Original Transmission: Sunday 13th May 1973 at 7.25 p.m.

The standard of cooking and hygiene at the depot canteen is abysmal and the staff demand changes. Jack threatens to call his members out on strike, leaving Blakey and the new Area Manager with a problem. Matters get worse when the cook resigns, and it is left to the Inspector to find a replacement. He finds a solution close at hand in the form of Mrs Butler.

An interview at the depot turns out to be a formality, as the Area Manager happens to be an old flame of Mrs Butler's from many years ago. It soon becomes clear that the Area Manager, Gerald, and Mabel Butler have warm feelings for each other, and Jack sees this as an opportunity to gain favours with the management and hold power over Blakey.

The Inspector is boxed into a corner and has to make concessions. He also finds himself dealt smaller portions in the canteen compared with Olive and Jack, but he has no say as they have friends in high places. Relief is soon at hand for the hapless Inspector, however, as he is told that Gerald is to retire and move away from Luxton. Jack's power is lost and the balance of control is back with Inspector Blake.

CAST:

Jack	Bob Grant
Olive	Anna Karen
Inspector	Stephen Lewis
Mum	Doris Hare
Mr Simpson	Bob Todd
Mrs Webb	Claire Davenport
Alf	Albert Moses

STORIES EDITED BY:	Ronald Wolfe and Ronald Chesney
DESIGNER:	Alan Hunter-Craig
PRODUCER:	Bryan Izzard

Series 7, Episode 13 – 'Gardening Time'
Written by Bob Grant and Stephen Lewis
Original Transmission: Sunday 20th May 1973 at 7.25 p.m.

The manager organises a gardening competition and Blakey sees it as a chance to gain favour with his boss. Jack also plans to enter, but his motivation is the prize money on offer to the winner. Unfortunately, Jack has never been green-fingered and his garden needs a lot of work to stand any chance. Blakey isn't any better off either, as the Butler's back garden resembles a rubbish tip, much to the glee of Jack next door.

The competition begins to hot up when Jack helps himself to flower arrangements on public display, which he passes while on duty. Blakey is also busy buying plants, but he runs into problems when boarding Jack's bus.

As judgement day nears, the pair can't resist resorting to dirty tricks to improve their chances of winning. Jack sets his pet cat loose in Blakey's garden and he responds by sabotaging Jack's flower display, running the risk of ruining both gardens. Worse is to come for poor Inspector Blake, but who will win the gardening contest?

CAST:

Jack	Bob Grant
Olive	Anna Karen
Inspector	Stephen Lewis
Mum	Doris Hare
Sandra	Sandra Bryant
Manager	Michael Sheard
Fred	Larry Martyn
Policeman	Ivor Salter
Rag and Bone Man	Ernest Jennings
Tibbles	Tiberius Grant

STORIES EDITED BY:	Ronald Wolfe and Ronald Chesney
DESIGNER:	Rodney Cammish
PRODUCER:	Bryan Izzard

CREW DETAILS

The Writers
RONALD WOLFE AND RONALD CHESNEY

Debut On The Buses Script: Series 1, Episode 1: 'The Early Shift'
On The Buses Episode Scripts: 54
On The Buses Film Scripts: 3

Scriptwriting Career

The highly successful writing partnership of Ronald Wolfe and Ronald Chesney was formed in the early 1950s. Their first venture was to provide scripts for comedy shows broadcast on BBC radio and their talents were soon elevated onto the television stage.

In 1958 Wolfe and Chesney wrote scripts for an ITV comedy called Educating Archie, which ran for 13 episodes and centred on a ventriloquist and his dummy. Wolfe and Chesney were not the sole contributors for this series, however, as multi-talented Marty Feldman and writer Barry Pevan also contributed. Educating Archie's other claim to fame is that it starred comedy greats Dick Emery and Irene Handl.

Wolfe and Chesney's next piece of work was for the BBC and provided them with one of their biggest hits. Based in the fictional Fenner Fashions fabrics factory, The Rag Trade began in 1961 and ran for three series and thirty-six episodes. It tackled the power struggle between management and the unions (a trait of On The Buses) and proved to be a huge success. Penned entirely by Wolfe and Chesney, it also boasted a cast of high pedigree including Reg Varney, Miriam Karlin, Esma Cannon, Sheila Hancock, Barbara Windsor and Peter Jones, among others. The Rag Trade ended in 1963 but was resurrected over a decade later.

Sitcoms were now being churned out frequently and to a high standard by Wolfe and Chesney, and next to hit our screens was Meet the Wife. This BBC sitcom followed a married couple (played by Thora Hird and Freddie Finton), portraying the wife as snobby and bossy and always wielding power over her downtrodden husband. Meet the Wife ran for five series and thirty-nine episodes between 1963 and 1966.

The writing duo's success was not only restricted to British television, however. In 1964 their scripts appeared on Australian television in the form of a sitcom called Barley Charlie, which followed two sisters attempting to run a dilapidated roadhouse and garage that they had inherited. The sitcom ran for one series of thirteen episodes.

The Two Writing Ronnies, as they have been called in some quarters, were to take another new step in their career in 1965 when they wrote the script for the film I've Gotta Horse, which combined the comedy talents of Michael Medwin, Bill Fraser and Peter Gilmore, among others, with musicians of the calibre of Billy Fury and The Bachelors to create a musical comedy. It was a pleasant mix and would not be the last big-screen effort by Wolfe and Chesney.

Around the same time as I've Gotta Horse was hitting the cinemas a BBC sitcom called The Bed-Sit Girl was first aired. The plot followed a typist who shared a bedsit with a flatmate that led a more exciting life. Sheila Hancock starred (working with Wolfe and Chesney scripts again) alongside Dilys Laye, Hy Hazell and Derek Nimmo. The Bed-Sit Girl ran for twelve episodes in two series from 1965 to 1966.

A year later, in 1967, Wolfe and Chesney's next sitcom was aired by the BBC. Sorry I'm Single featured Gwendolyn Watts (who went on to appear in two episodes of On The Buses) as Brenda, a divorcee on the lookout for another husband, and co-starred Derek Nimmo and Elizabeth Knight. Unfortunately, the series did not take off and ran for just one series and nine episodes.

Another BBC sitcom called According to Dora benefited from the Two Ronnies' input, but the scripts for the fifteen episodes were supplied by an army of scriptwriters. The sitcom, aired in 1968, oozed a castful of comedy legends such as Dora Bryan, Wilfrid Brambell, Kenneth Connor, Clive Dunn and Joan Sims.

In the first few days of 1969 the BBC brought to our screens another Wolfe and Chesney creation, a one-series comedy called Wild, Wild Women, which followed a similar storyline to their earlier classic The Rag Trade. Set in a factory in Edwardian times, it followed the female workers' conflicts with management, and the cast included Anna Karen (soon to become a household name in On The Buses). The series was decommissioned after the six-episode run.

No sooner had Wild, Wild Women finished its short stint when along came the Wolfe and Chesney masterpiece On The Buses. For their scripts to come to fruition they took the idea to LWT (London Weekend Television), and the rest is history. On The Buses ran for seven series and seventy-four episodes, fifty-four of which were penned by Wolfe and Chesney, and the classic sitcom was to win an award for its excellence during its run from 1969 to 1973.

Reg Varney had worked closely with Wolfe and Chesney scripts in the form of The Rag Trade and On The Buses and was to do so again in 1970. His sketch show The Other Reg Varney presented him with the opportunity to display his other talents such as playing the piano. The one-off show was also penned by Reg Varney and Peter Dulay.

In 1971 the Wolfe and Chesney partnership wrote the script for and produced the spin-off film On The Buses, starring the cast of the TV series and joined by Andrea

Lawrence, Pat Ashton, Brian Oulton, Pat Coombs and Wendy Richard, to name but a few. The film became a smash hit and was the top earner at the box office in 1971, just beating the James Bond film Diamonds Are Forever to the top spot.

Just under a year later the Wolfe and Chesney team wrote the scripts for Mutiny On The Buses, which saw the return of the regular cast joined by Pat Ashton, Janet Mahoney, Kevin Brennan and David Lodge, among others. The film was another lucrative earner at the box office and is still enjoyed by the fans today.

Also in 1972, back on the small screen, a sitcom appeared called Romany Jones, another LWT production. To be fair, it was not Wolfe and Chesney's most noted work. The storylines centred around a family of gypsies living on a caravan site and starred Arthur Mullard, Queenie Watts, James Beck and Jonathan Cecil. Although criticised by some, Romany Jones ran for four series and twenty-seven episodes from 1972 to 1975.

The third and final On The Buses spin-off film came in 1973, again written by Wolfe and Chesney, and took the team away from the bus depot to a holiday camp. Holiday On The Buses saw the return of Michael Robbins and Reg Varney to the cast, despite their having left the TV series before it had run its course, and also starred Wilfrid Brambell, Kate Williams, Arthur Mullard, Queenie Watts, Henry McGhee and Hal Dyer. As with the previous films it claimed very respectable box office receipts, and it was rated by many fans as their favourite film of the trilogy.

With On The Buses assigned to television history when it ended in 1973, the next project for the writing talents of Wolfe and Chesney was to pen the scripts for an On The Buses spin-off series. Don't Drink the Water followed the life of Cyril Blake, who retired as Inspector and moved to a villa in Spain with his sister. Stephen Lewis reprised his role, and his screen sister, Dorothy, was played by Pat Coombs. It failed to reach the popularity of On The Buses, running for two series and thirteen episodes from 1974 to 1975, and was panned by critics. Since it was originally aired it has been criminally deprived of any repeats on television.

Wolfe and Chesney's next piece of work was another spin-off. In 1976 Yus My Dear hit the screens, which was a sequel to their earlier sitcom Romany Jones. Arthur Mullard and Queenie Watts reprised their roles as the gypsy couple, Mr and Mrs Briggs, and they were joined by stand-up comedian Mike Reid. Although the first series attracted good viewing figures, its popularity evaporated for the second series and so, after mixed fortunes and nineteen episodes, LWT pulled the plug.

A one-off comedy written by the Two Writing Ronnies called The Boys and Mrs B was aired on BBC1 in 1977. This starred Thora Hird, Gordon Kaye and Richard Caldicot but it never went any further than the pilot episode.

Later in 1977 came the resurrection of The Rag Trade, fourteen years after it had last aired on the BBC. Now an LWT production, this sitcom saw Anna Karen reprise her character Olive, joined by the only surviving members of the original cast, Peter Jones and Miriam Karlin. The rebirth of The Rag Trade lasted for two series and twenty-two episodes, running from 1977 to 1978, and even though it failed to draw the same large viewing figures as the original series it is still fondly remembered.

There was to be a two-year gap before another Wolfe and Chesney sitcom hit our screens. Aired on the BBC in early 1980, Watch this Space followed the exploits of an advertising agency and starred Liza Goddard, Christopher Biggins and Peter Blake, but it ran for only six episodes.

Similarly, a year later in 1981, the duo wrote a sitcom for

Southern Television (part of the ITV network) called Take a Letter Mr Jones, which only ran the course of one six-episode series before its demise. The plot focused on a case of role-reversal, featuring a top female business executive faced with the sexual politics of her business and staff ineptness and assisted by her male secretary. Take a Letter Mr Jones starred Rula Lenska and John Inman and it was to spell the end of an era, as it was the last Wolfe and Chesney sitcom to make it onto British television.

Their scriptwriting careers were far from over, however, and in 1989 they penned an episode of the smash hit Jeremy Lloyd and David Croft sitcom 'Allo 'Allo! called 'The Big Flush'. This was followed a year later by a venture into Scandinavian television using a tried and trusted plotline. Wolfe and Chesney wrote a Swedish adaptation of The Rag Trade called Fredriksson's fabrikk, which ran from 1990 to 1993 and proved popular in Scandinavia. It even spawned a spin-off film in 1994, the script co-written by Wolfe and Chesney and Swede Andreas Markusson. This was the last piece of work penned by the Two Writing Ronnies to make it onto film.

The Ronald Wolfe/Ronald Chesney partnership is one of the longest running in British television history. It spanned five decades and spawned numerous sitcoms with varying degrees of success, stretching to continents all around the world. Their work is still treasured by fans of comedy and is constantly winning new generations of fans many years after they penned their final sitcom.

FILMOGRAPHY

Film

I've Gotta Horse (1965)
On The Buses (1971)
Mutiny On The Buses (1972)

Holiday On The Buses (1973)
Fredriksson's fabrikk (1994)

Television
Educating Archie (1958)
The Rag Trade (1961-1963)
Comedy Playhouse (1963-1968)
Meet the Wife (1964-1966)
Barley Charlie (1964)
The Bed-Sit Girl (1965-1966)
Sorry I'm Single (1967)
According to Dora (1968-1969)
Wild, Wild Women (1969)
On The Buses (1969-1973)
The Reg Varney Revue (1970)
Romany Jones (1972-1975)
Don't Drink the Water (1974-1975)
Yus My Dear (1976)
The Boys and Mrs B. (1977)
The Rag Trade (1977-1978)
Watch This Space (1980)
Take a Letter Mr Jones (1981)
'Allo 'Allo (1989)
Fredriksson's fabrikk (1990)
Freddytex (1994)

BOB GRANT AND STEPHEN LEWIS

Debut On The Buses Script: Series 5, Episode 13: 'Vacancy for Inspector'
On The Buses Episode Scripts: 12

Scriptwriting Career

Bob Grant and Stephen Lewis were not only highly talented

comedy actors but also very accomplished scriptwriters. They had worked together as part of the On The Buses cast since 1969, and in early 1970 their first scripts made it onto television. The long-running BBC series Comedy Playhouse used a Grant and Lewis script called The Jugg Brothers, which starred both Bob Grant and Stephen Lewis, who played the part of brothers.

When Ronald Wolfe and Ronald Chesney took more of a back seat as scriptwriters for On The Buses it was Bob Grant and Stephen Lewis who took up the role. From 1971 to 1973 they wrote a total of 12 episodes, stretching over the last three series. It was a hard task, as they had to contend with the loss of two key cast members, Michael Robbins and Reg Varney, but it was to their credit that they supplied high-quality scripts that ensured the continued success of On The Buses.

FILMOGRAPHY
Television
Comedy Playhouse (1970)
On The Buses (1971-1973)

GEORGE LAYTON AND JONATHAN LYNN

Debut On The Buses Script: Series 6, Episode 2: 'Love is What You Make It'
On The Buses Episode Scripts: 6

Scriptwriting Career

The highly regarded writing partnership of George Layton and Jonathan Lynn was similar in many ways to that of Bob Grant and Stephen Lewis in that they were both talented comedy actors who had worked alongside each other in the hit sitcom Doctor in the House. The Layton and Lynn partnership wrote episodes for a number of sitcoms spanning a number of years.

They first combined their writing talents when they supplied a script for an episode of Doctor at Large in 1971. This was soon to be followed by their penning six episodes of On The Buses, spread over the last two series from 1972 to 1973. They contributed scripts for another Wolfe and Chesney sitcom in 1973 when they wrote an episode for Romany Jones. Also at this time they wrote eleven episodes for the two series of the latest incarnation of the long-running 'Doctor' series of sitcoms called Doctor in Charge. A year later, in 1974, Layton and Lynn penned four episodes of the spin-off Doctor at Sea, which followed two out-of-work doctors who sign up to work aboard a cruise ship as medical officers.

A short-lived sitcom called My Name is Harry Worth was aired on ITV in 1974. The Thames Television production, which starred Harry Worth, ran for a mere eight episodes, three of which were penned by Layton and Lynn.

In 1975 the duo returned to work on a spin-off sitcom, writing five episodes of the first series of Doctor on the Go, which starred Robin Nedwell, Geoffrey Davies and Ernest Clark. This LWT production ran for two series from 1975 to 1977 and was yet another quality sitcom in the long-running saga, which had featured three spin-offs from the original series.

It was in 1975 that Layton and Lynn wrote their first sitcom together, My Brother's Keeper, in which they both starred as twin brothers. The sitcom, a Granada production aired on ITV, ran for just one thirteen-episode series from 1975 to 1976. This proved to be the final piece of work written by the partnership, as subsequently they went their separate ways. Both men continued scriptwriting in their own right with great success, creating sitcoms such as Executive Stress (written by Layton) and Yes Minister and Yes Prime Minister (written by Lynn), as well as writing scripts for films.

FILMOGRAPHY
Television
Doctor at Large (1971)
On The Buses (1972-1973)
Doctor in Charge (1972-1973)
Romany Jones (1973)
Doctor at Sea (1974)
My Name is Harry Worth (1974)
Doctor on the Go (1975)
My Brother's Keeper (1975-1976)

WALLY MALSTON AND GARRY CHAMBERS

Debut On The Buses Script: Series 7, Episode 4: 'The Poster'
On The Buses Episode Scripts: 1

Scriptwriting Career

The scriptwriting team of Wally Malston and Garry Chambers first came together in 1972. Wally Malston had the experience of having written material for the children's hit series Crackerjack while Garry Chambers had yet to see any of his work reach the screens. In the early autumn of 1972 they had the distinction of writing material for the legendary comedy double act of Ronnie Barker and Ronnie Corbett, and Malston and Chambers' material appeared in five episodes of The Two Ronnies from 1972 to 1973. Towards the end of 1972 they combined again to write material for the LWT variety show The Reg Varney Revue, which starred Reg Varney and ran for six episodes.

A few months later, in 1973, Malston and Chambers penned their only episode of On The Buses. 'The Poster' featured in the final series and was rated favourably by fans of the sitcom. In 1974 the pair wrote material for Reg Varney's latest show, unimaginatively named Reg Varney, which ran for six episodes. This was to be the last time the two writers worked together, but both continued to write scripts for a number of classic television shows such as 3-2-1, The Les Dawson Show, Russ Abbot's Madhouse and Noel's House Party.

FILMOGRAPHY
Television
The Two Ronnies (1972-1973)
The Reg Varney Revue (1972)
On The Buses (1973)
Reg Varney (1974)

MILES RUDGE

Debut On The Buses Script: Series 7, Episode 11: 'The Allowance'
On The Buses Episode Scripts: 1

Scriptwriting Career
Miles Rudge started out in show business as an actor but soon realised that he possessed a better talent for writing. He began penning scripts for radio shows in the 1950s and also wrote hit singles for none other than Bernard Cribbins. His first venture into television came in 1962 when some of his material was used in the BBC drama Compact, which ran for twenty-three episodes over two series from 1962 to 1965. Also in 1962 he scripted an episode of the BBC sitcom Brothers in Law, which starred Richard Briers, among others.

There was to be an eight-year gap before another Miles Rudge script made it onto television. The BBC's Comedy Playhouse series provided us with an episode called 'An Officer and a Gentleman', which starred Patricia Hayes and

James Grout.

In 1973 Miles Rudge wrote his only episode of On The Buses, 'The Allowance', which featured in the final series and guest-starred Yootha Joyce. This was the only episode of the sitcom to be written by a single scriptwriter rather than a partnership.

Rudge also wrote three episodes of the lesser-known Wolfe and Chesney sitcom Romany Jones from 1973 to 1974. This was to be his last television script for eight years, until he wrote his own sitcom.

In 1982 he co-wrote the ITV sitcom Father Charlie alongside the legendary Vince Powell (creator of many classic sitcoms). Father Charlie was based around a nuns' convent and their new chaplain, who was played by the great comedy actor Lionel Jeffries. This Central Television production never took off, running for just six episodes, and these scripts proved to be the final ones written by Miles Rudge for television.

FILMOGRAPHY

Television

Compact (1962)
Brothers in Law (1962)
Comedy Playhouse (1970)
On The Buses (1973)
Romany Jones (1973-1974)
Father Charlie (1982)

THE PRODUCERS

STUART ALLEN

Debut On The Buses Production: Series 1, Episode 1: 'The Early Shift'
On The Buses Episodes Produced: 39

Career as a Producer
The name Stuart Allen is synonymous with the production of hit British sitcoms. His career as producer began in 1966 when he produced an episode of Comedy Playhouse for the BBC called 'The Bishop Rides Again'. This was to blossom into the highly rated BBC sitcom All Gas and Gaiters and starred Derek Nimmo, William Mervyn and Joan Sanderson, among others. Stuart Allen was responsible for the production of the whole seven-episode first series from 1966 to 1967 before moving on to his next project. All Gas and Gaiters went on to reach high acclaim, but sadly none of the episodes remain in existence, as the videotapes were wiped a number of years ago.

After producing a rather nondescript sitcom called Ooh La La, which it is fair to say wasn't his biggest success, Stuart Allen joined London Weekend Television. He produced the one-off comedy Mrs Wilson's Diary, which starred On The Buses legends Stephen Lewis and Bob Grant and was based on a stage show's satirical look at life in 10 Downing Street.

It was in 1969 that Stuart Allen became the first producer of LWT's new sitcom On The Buses and he remained in that post throughout the first four series. He worked on many of the best episodes that made it a smash-hit sitcom and left the post with the show at the height of its popularity.

Early in 1971 Allen left On The Buses, but another hit sitcom was just around the corner in the form of Thames Television's Love Thy Neighbour, starring Jack Smethurst, Rudolph Walker, Kate Williams and Nina Baden-Powell. Although it proved to be a very controversial sitcom, it was a hit with the British viewing public. The plot centred around culturally diverse next-door neighbours involved in constant conflict, and critics labelled the sitcom as racist due to its content. In today's age of political correctness it is unlikely that Love Thy Neighbour will ever be repeated on British television, but it still has a legion of fans. In 1972 Allen produced the first two series of the sitcom, comprising thirteen episodes.

The next project for Stuart Allen was another new LWT sitcom called Billy Liar. Based on the Keith Waterhouse novel of the same name, the sitcom follows a young man from the north-east of England who lives his life in a daydream. It is still highly rated in many quarters even though it has not been screened for many years, and it ran for two series produced entirely by Stuart Allen.

Also on Allen's CV is the Ronald Wolfe and Ronald Chesney sitcom Romany Jones, which ran from 1972 to 1975 over four series and twenty-seven episodes, all produced and directed by Stuart Allen. This was followed by a spin-off Wolfe and Chesney sitcom called Yus My Dear, which aired in 1976 and ran for two series.

Stuart Allen had the honour of producing the first episode of a new LWT sitcom in 1975 called Two's Company, which starred Donald Sinden and Elaine Stritch. It went on to be a big success, with Humphrey Barclay taking on the producing role after the first episode. Also with LWT in 1976 came a sitcom called The Fosters, which focused on the life of the Foster family from South London and starred a young actor called Lenny Henry. The sitcom ran for two series and twenty-seven episodes, each of which were produced by Allen.

The much sought-after producer's next hit sitcom was the ATV production A Sharp Intake of Breath, starring comedy greats David Jason and Richard Wilson. Its plot involved a young married couple, with husband (David Jason) and wife forced to deal with the mishaps of life. A largely forgotten sitcom but held in high regard, it ran for four series from 1977 to 1981 and was co-produced by Stuart Allen and Les Chatfield.

Also in 1977 a Thames Television sitcom called The Fuzz, starring Lynda Bellingham and On The Buses star Michael Robbins and based around policemen in a quiet police station, hit our television screens. All seven episodes were produced by Stuart Allen, but the series failed to make an impact and went no further than one series. In the same year Allen worked on a Wolfe and Chesney sitcom for the fourth and last time in his career. The rebirth of The Rag Trade, which ran for two series with mild success, was jointly produced by Stuart Allen and William G. Stewart and had another On The Buses connection in the form of Anna Karen, who reprised her role of Olive in the show.

At the end of 1977 the latest LWT sitcom Mind Your Language aired for the first time, with Stuart Allen as producer. The sitcom followed a teacher's attempts to teach a class of multinational adults to speak English. Much like Love Thy Neighbour it is now frowned upon as being xenophobic and bordering on racist in the politically correct world of today, but it was a big hit when it first hit our screens. Mind Your Language ran for four series from 1977 to 1986, with Stuart Allen producing the first three series and directing the final one.

Another much-loved sitcom began in 1980. The BBC comedy Yes Minister, starring Paul Eddington, Nigel Hawthorne and Derek Fowlds, openly poked fun at the world of British politics. The very first episode, 'Open Government', was produced by Stuart Allen and was the only episode in the entire three series that he worked on.

A chance to work with legendary actor Sir John Mills was afforded to Allen in 1980. The sitcom Young at Heart, an ATV production, was written by the famous comedy writer Vince Powell and the plotline revolved around a man who is forced against his wishes to retire at the age of sixty-five. Sir John Mills starred alongside Meg Jenkins, but despite running for three series and spawning nineteen episodes from 1980 to 1982, all produced by Stuart Allen, the sitcom was not a major success.

Another ATV sitcom came along in 1981, produced by Allen. Doctor's Daughters was loosely connected with the Doctor in the House series and was based around the lives of three elderly doctors. Unfortunately it proved to be a flop and survived no more than six episodes before it was axed.

A year later, in 1982, a new sitcom called Father Charlie first aired. However, despite being written by Vince Powell, produced by Stuart Allen and starring Lionel Jeffries, it was destined to fail. It ran for just six episodes before being dropped from the schedules and assigned to television history.

Another short-lived sitcom produced by Allen was next on the agenda. Jack of Diamonds was aired on the BBC, was based around a detective agency and starred comedy legend Dick Emery, Tony Selby and Glynn Edwards. The sitcom ran for six episodes and was co-produced by Harold Snoad.

Stuart Allen's last project as a producer came in 1984 after three decades of working in television production. It was fitting that he should end his career at London Weekend Television, which had given him his greatest successes with the likes of On The Buses and Mind Your Language.

Unfortunately, however, there was no fairy-tale ending, in fact quite the opposite. The sitcom Bottle Boys centred on a randy, football-mad milkman's exploits and those of his multinational fellow milkmen and starred Robin Askwith (who was made famous by his appearances in the bawdy 1970s 'Confessions' sex-comedy film series). Bottle Boys ran for two series and thirteen episodes, but critics and the vast majority of the viewing public alike panned it and it is often rated as one of the worst sitcoms of all time. It was a sad end to the illustrious producing career of Stuart Allen.

FILMOGRAPHY

Television

Comedy Playhouse (1966)
All Gas and Gaiters (1967)
Ooh La La (1968)
Never a Cross Word (1968)
Mrs Wilson's Diary (1969)
On The Buses (1969-1971)
Mike and Bernie (1971-1972)
Romany Jones (1972-1975)
Love Thy Neighbour (1972)
Billy Liar (1973-1974)
Two's Company (1975)
The Fosters (1976-1977)
Yus My Dear (1976)
A Sharp Intake of Breath (1977-1981)
The Fuzz (1977)
The Rag Trade (1977-1978)
Mind Your Language (1977-1986)
Yes Minister (1980)
Young at Heart (1980)
Doctor's Daughters (1981)
Father Charlie (1982)

Jack of Diamonds (1983)
Bottle Boys (1984-1985)

DERRICK GOODWIN

Debut On The Buses Production: Series 5, Episode 1: 'The Nursery'
On The Buses Episodes Produced: 18

Career as a Producer

Producer Derrick Goodwin could not have been handed a more daunting start to his career in that field. When Stuart Allen stepped down from the position of producer of On The Buses at the end of the fourth series the sitcom was flying high in the ratings. It was Derrick Goodwin's task as the next producer to maintain its standing as a classic sitcom, and he did an admirable job. He ended up in charge of the production of the entire fifth series and an end total of eighteen episodes, from 1971 to 1972.

Goodwin remained at London Weekend Television after his spell as producer of On The Buses and went on to produce the sitcom The Train Now Standing, which revolved around a railway stationmaster working in a quiet run-down train station. It starred Ronald Fraser, Pamela Cundell and Norman Mitchell and ran for two series and fifteen episodes from 1972 to 1973, all of them produced by Goodwin. Unfortunately it was not a great hit with the viewers.

Still with LWT, in 1973 Goodwin was co-producer of the sitcom Bowler, which was a spin-off to the better-known comedy The Fenn Street Gang and followed a wealthy crook who just wanted to be accepted by upper-class society. It starred George Baker in the lead role, but it was destined for the chop after one series of pretty ordinary comedy for that era.

Goodwin's next project was the LWT sitcom Thick as

Thieves in 1974. Penned by writing legends Dick Clement and Ian La Frenais, the plot centred on two crooks living together (played by Bob Hoskins and John Thaw). The sitcom showed much promise but was axed after the eight episodes of the first series.

After a gap of four years away from producing, Goodwin returned in 1978 to produce the mildly successful sitcom Mixed Blessings. The comedy focused on a mixed-race couple's marriage and the obstacles they faced when their relationship was frowned upon by relatives. It wasn't the only sitcom of that era to tackle racial attitudes and relationships but it did so without causing any real controversy in the public eye. Mixed Blessings starred Christopher Blake and Muriel Odunton and ran for three series and twenty-two episodes from 1978 to 1980.

In the spring of 1979 Goodwin's next production project was Lovely Couple. Sadly, this sitcom failed to register with the viewing public and after a thirteen-episodes first series it was scrapped. Goodwin's career with LWT continued and in 1980 a sitcom called Holding the Fort hit our screens, which starred a pre-Doctor Who Peter Davison. Unfortunately, it did not make it past the first series, which ran for seven episodes.

At least Goodwin's following sitcom, Now and Then, progressed into a second series. The comedy was written by the accomplished team of John Esmonde and Bob Larbey (creators of hit sitcom Please Sir!) and ran for two series. However, it is not held in high esteem and is a much-forgotten sitcom.

Goodwin's following sitcom was a short-lived affair. The Kit Curran Radio Show featured an anarchic radio station DJ who was determined to do things his way against the wishes of his bosses. Six episodes later the sitcom ended.

In 1987 came another LWT sitcom about an ageing man

longing for life as it used to be in his youth. Running Wild starred Ray Brooks, Janet Key and Michelle Collins and ran for two series, gaining mixed reviews. Derrick Goodwin and Marcus Plantin co-produced the thirteen episodes. The same year saw Goodwin produce Ffizz, a sitcom based around a pair of wine merchants who loved living the high life but were forced to find work when they lost their wealth. Richard Griffiths and Benjamin Whitrow played the starring roles, and although the sitcom is largely overlooked it does get some favourable reviews from viewers. It ran for two series from 1987 to 1989 and was produced entirely by Goodwin.

This was to be his final notable project as a producer in a career spanning thirty years. It began with On The Buses and I think it is fair to say that his role in its production was the pinnacle of his career.

FILMOGRAPHY

Television

On The Buses (1971-1972)
The Train Now Standing (1973)
Bowler (1973)
Thick as Thieves (1974)
Mixed Blessings (1978-1980)
Lovely Couple (1979)
Holding the Fort (1980)
Fancy Wanders (1980)
Now and Then (1983-1984)
The Kit Curran Radio Show (1984)
Mann's Best Friends (1985)
South of the Border (1985)
Running Wild (1987-1989)
Ffizz (1987-1989)
Taking the Floor (1991)

BRYAN IZZARD

Debut On The Buses Production: Series 6, Episode 2: 'Love is What You Make It'
On The Buses Episodes Produced: 17

Career as a Producer

Bryan Izzard's producing career began at London Weekend Television in 1970 with a comedy sketch show starring the rising young star Kenny Everett. The series, called Making Whoopee, ran for six episodes before its demise. As we all know, Kenny Everett went on to bigger and better things, but not before featuring in another series in 1970 called Ev, which ran for nine episodes from 1970 to 1971 and was also produced by Izzard.

His first venture into the realm of sitcoms came when he produced five episodes of the hit spin-off sitcom The Fenn Street Gang from 1971 to 1972. The comedy was penned by John Esmonde and Bob Larbey, and although it may not be as fondly remembered as its predecessor Please Sir! it is still a quality sitcom that followed the lives of ex-pupils from Fenn Street School.

It was at the start of 1972 that Bryan Izzard became the third and final producer of On The Buses. He produced seventeen episodes in total, including some great storylines, in the sixth and seventh series. Izzard was somewhat handicapped in his task, as the great cast began to split up, so credit is due to him for managing to maintain a good standard of quality. Towards the end of 1972 he worked with Reg Varney again, producing all six episodes of the comedy sketch and variety show The Reg Varney Revue, which featured guest appearances from stars such as Pat Coombs, David Lodge, Frank Thornton and The Osmonds.

Still with LWT, Izzard's next project was working on another hit sitcom called Not on Your Nellie. Hylda Baker starred

Left: The site of the fictional Luxton and District Bus Depot

Below: The redevelopement is evident on Lordship Lane.

Above: The Cemetery Gates as they are today

Right: A view from the west end of Cedar Road across to where we often saw Stan's bus parked

Above: The traffic island in which we see Stan, Jack and Blakey aboard the motorcyle combination rounding.

Right: Stan's bus breaks down at this location with a bed aboard as well as four trainees

Left: Blakey is carried away by a runaway piano on this street

Below: Stan crashed his bus into a garden but they no longer exist being replaced by concrete

Above: The Butler house as it looks today

Right: The tree that Blakey hides behind still stands as can be seen on the right

Above: The scene of the closing credits sequence in Series 7

Right: Here once stood Stage 5 of Elstree Studios which doubled as the Bus Depot

Left: The Butler house as seen in all three spin-off films with the set of EastEnders visible to the right

Below: The Launderette remains in business to the present day

Above: Betty's House - The upstairs bedroom was actually used in filming as well

Right: Stan's bus comes to a halt here and he shouts: 'Jump on Mum'

Above: The site as it looks today with a new fence and hedge now present where the sidecar came to rest

Right: The location of Arthur's driving lessons and Stan and Jack's darts practice.

Left: This distinctive hilly road was ideal for a runaway sidecar scene

Below: The entrance into Pontins Prestatyn Holiday Park today and clear to see little has changed

Above: Crash barriers now align the bridge that spans the River Clwyd

Right: In Holiday On The Buses Stan urges his passengers to board the bus and these two distinctive houses can be seen in the background

Above: Olive exits this shop holding sticks of candy floss

Right: Stan drives his bus across this bridge at Foryd Harbour in Rhyl

as a teetotaller who moved from Yorkshire to London to help run her father's pub. Although it is never repeated on British television it is still held in high regard by many and reviews are good. Not on Your Nellie ran for three series and seventeen episodes, all produced by Bryan Izzard, from 1974 to 1975.

Although he was kept busy directing a whole host of well-known television shows, Izzard's next notable piece of work as a producer came in 1979, five years after Not on Your Nellie. The STV (Scottish Television) production The Allan Stewart Tapes was a five-episode comedy sketch show featuring Scottish impressionist Allan Stewart and 'Carry On' star Jack Douglas.

During his career Izzard also produced drama series such as Charles Endell Esq. and Together, but he will be best remembered for the sitcoms. Sadly, his next sitcom was not one of his production successes. Take a Letter Mr Jones, written by Ronald Wolfe and Ronald Chesney, was axed after six episodes although to be fair it is not the worst sitcom ever. Another rather less than successful sitcom followed in 1982 called Rep. This Granada Television offering, which ran for a mere four episodes, featured On The Buses star Stephen Lewis, 'Carry On' star Patsy Rowlands and Iain Cuthbertson.

After an eight-year retirement from the producer's chair Izzard returned to ply his trade at the BBC. In 1991 a series of plays written by Noel Coward were aired under the title of Tonight at 8.30 and boasted casts of high pedigree, with Joan Collins, Anthony Newley, John Alderton and none other than Reg Varney making an appearance. The eight plays were produced by Bryan Izzard and Joan Collins.

Also in 1991 came a BBC sitcom called An Actor's Life for Me, which marked the winding up of Izzard's producing career. The plot involved a struggling actor's desperate attempts to reach stardom, and the lengths he was prepared to go to and the roles he took on provide the laughs. It starred John Gordon-Sinclair, Gina McKee and comedy great Victor Spinetti and is seen as a much-underrated sitcom even though it only ran for one series of six episodes. An Actor's Life for Me was a respectable way for Bryan Izzard to sign off his career after over twenty years in the trade, having produced a number of hit sitcoms and having worked with the biggest and best comedy actors of that time.

FILMOGRAPHY

Television

Making Whoopee (1970)
Ev (1970-1971)
The Fenn Street Gang (1971-1972)
On The Buses (1972-1973)
The Reg Varney Revue (1972)
Not on Your Nellie (1974-1975)
Out With the Old, In With the New (1978)
The Allan Stewart Tapes (1978)
Charles Endell Esq. (1979)
Together (1980)
Take a Letter Mr Jones (1981)
Rep (1982)
Here's a Funny Thing (1982)
Interference (1983)
Tonight at 8.30 (1991)
An Actor's Life for Me (1991)

FILMING LOCATIONS

Television Series

For many years the filming locations used in the On The Buses TV series have been shrouded in mystery, but in recent months a handful have been unearthed and confirmed. It is evident that the production crew never travelled too far from the studios for its location shoots. Logistics determined that equipment and crew were very expensive to transport and so it must have made perfect sense to keep the filming on location in close proximity to the studios.

When On The Buses first hit our screens in 1969 it was filmed at the leased home of London Weekend Television, Wembley Studios. Filming locations tended to be confined to areas north of the River Thames within reasonable distance of the studios. The first six series were filmed at Wembley Studios, which amounted to sixty-one episodes.

It was late in 1972 that LWT moved into their new custom-built studios. South Bank Studios were located on the south side of the banks of the River Thames. The seventh series of On The Buses was filmed at the South Bank Studios, but this brought with it a problem. Unlike at Wembley Studios, the famous Bristol Lodekka FLFs were unable to gain entrance to the mock bus depot inside the studios, as the entrance doors into the studio were just too small. To work around this problem single-decker buses were used and plywood imitation second decks were lowered from the lighting rig onto each bus.

In total thirteen episodes were filmed at the South Bank Studios, and the filming locations for those episodes were confined to an area south of the River Thames within a few miles' radius of the studios.

As to the exact locations used for filming the outdoor scenes of On The Buses, a selection of these will be revealed in the next section.

The Bus Depot

The fictional Luxton and District Traction Company's bus depot featured in many episodes of On The Buses. The interior scenes at the depot were filmed at LWT's Wembley Studios, but the exterior shots were filmed on location at an actual active bus depot. External shots of buses entering and exiting the depot were filmed at what was then the Eastern National's Wood Green depot situated on Lordship Lane in Wood Green, North London.

Sadly, the depot was demolished shortly after its closure in 1981. The land was redeveloped and a DIY store was built on the site of the old bus depot, to be replaced in the 1990s with a bingo hall. To this day a Mecca Bingo Hall remains on the site.

As can be seen in the photographs (in the image section in the centre of the book) of the location taken recently, the houses adjacent to the site of the former depot on Lordship Lane have remained much the same. Obvious changes are the increased volume of parked cars, the number of houses that have converted to double-glazed windows and the satellite dishes that now adorn a number of the residences. Looking along Lordship Lane towards the Wood Green tube station, it is evident that this area has been heavily redeveloped since On The Buses was filmed there. A host of new structures have been built, including a multi-screen cinema complex.

The Cemetery Gates

Aside from the Wood Green bus depot, the most frequently seen filming location in On The Buses is the famed cemetery gates site. It is mentioned throughout all seven series and is the destination for Stan and Jack's No. 11 bus. We see the location in all its splendour for the first time in the Series 2 episode 'Bon Voyage' and again in the Series 3 episode 'First Aid', as well as other episodes.

The location of the cemetery gates can be found at Lavender Hill Cemetery, Cedar Road, Enfield, North London. As can be seen from the recent photographs (as seen in the image section) of the location (taken in late 2008), the area has remained much the same as it was when the On The Buses crew were frequent visitors in the late 1960s and early 1970s. There has been no redevelopment of the surrounding area in this quiet suburb of London, and a visit to this location is a very atmospheric and nostalgic experience for fans of the classic sitcom, as it is instantly recognisable as the hallowed cemetery gates filming location.

Series 3 – 'The Squeeze'

In a Series 3 episode called 'The Squeeze' we see another filming location when Stan and Jack attempt to sell Arthur's motorcycle combination to Blakey. They take the Inspector out for a test ride as a passenger in the sidecar and we see shots of the combination travelling down a quiet street lined with trees and upmarket houses.

This filming location is Dean Court, Brent, in Greater London. It was fairly local to the LWT Studios, which at that time were based at the Wembley Studios (now known as The Fountain Studios), being situated just over a mile-and-a-half to the west of the studios.

A present-day photograph (which can be seen in the image section) shows very little change when compared with the filming location. It would appear that the traffic island seen today has increased in size since On The Buses was filmed there. Also the pavements have been widened, in turn narrowing the road. The trees seen lining the road still exist to this day, and it is thought that the adjoining Stapenhill Road can also be seen in this episode.

Series 4 – 'The 'L' Bus'

In the episode called 'The 'L' Bus' we see Stan, Jack and their four trainees aboard a bus that breaks down. The bus comes to a halt and Stan gets out of his cab to see the engine suffering an oil leak.

The filming location of this scene has been tracked down and photographed and I can reveal that this scene was filmed in Wolves Lane, Tottenham, North London. To be precise, the bus stopped on the corner of the junction with Upsdell Avenue in Wolves Lane and the street signs can just be seen in the background in the episode.

The present-day photograph (in the image section in the centre pages) of this site show that it is largely unchanged. Obviously the invention of satellite television since the episode was filmed in 1970 has seen the erection of satellite dishes on a large number of the houses in Wolves Lane. It is also worth noting that the trees lining Upsdell Avenue seen in the episode are still present but of course have now grown somewhat. Apart from these minor changes the filming location has remained refreshingly similar.

Series 6 – 'Private Hire'

In the Series 6 episode called 'Private Hire' Stan and Jack take a bus out on tests, but in a desperate attempt to make some money they also use it as a removal van. When they are in the process of unloading a piano Blakey arrives on the scene to catch them in the act. This filming location has been tracked down and photographed recently.

The scene was filmed on Ferme Park Road, Hornsey, North London. As you can see from the episode scene, the bus stopped on a street at the top of a hill. The steep hill was crucial to the stunt that we see in the scene involving the runaway piano. In the distance, on top of a hill, Alexandra Palace is visible.

My visit to this filming location in December 2008 enabled me to photograph the site. As can be seen from the image in the centre pages, a lot of the adjacent houses have undergone loft conversions as well as having satellite dishes fitted. The traditional red post box seen in the episode still remains to this day.

Series 7 – 'The Poster'

The Series 7 episode called 'The Poster' contained a scene shot on location. The scene in question comes at the end of the episode when we see Stan driving his bus down a narrow street. He is distracted by one of the new promotional posters bearing his picture, which is being put up by the roadside, and crashes the depot's new bus into a small garden.

This filming location is in Gilbert Road, Lambeth, London, and is south of the River Thames. It is no more than a mile to the south-west of the South Bank Studios where at that time On The Buses was being filmed.

The photograph of the location as it looks today (which can be seen in the image section) show some subtle changes. The old buildings seen on the left of Gilbert Road in the episode have long since been demolished and a new housing estate now occupies that site. As for the row of houses with small gardens seen in the episode, they have also undergone slight changes. Although the houses themselves remain the same, the gardens no longer exist and the space they occupied has been concreted over, thus widening the pavement.

Series 7 – 'Hot Water'

In the Series 7 episode called 'Hot Water' a particular street is used as a filming location. The scene shows Blakey outside the Butler house with Jack and they are attempting to turn off the water at the stopcock in the street.

This scene was filmed outside 12, Carden Road, Southwark, South London. In terms of distance it was just under four-and-a-half miles south-east of the South Bank Studios. The surrounding areas of this location were used several times in the last few episodes ever made of On The Buses.

As can be seen from a recent photograph (in the image section in the centre pages) of this filming location, the houses remain largely unchanged. The house that doubled as the Butler residence has had a new door fitted and windows double-glazed. During the filming of On The Buses these houses had the customary metal dustbins outside, but now the street is lined with the modern-age wheelie bins. The manhole cover remains and can just be seen in the photograph.

Series 7 – 'The Allowance'

In the Series 7 episode called 'The Allowance' several scenes were shot on location. In one scene in particular we see clippie Sandra going into some public toilets, with Inspector Blake hiding behind a tree outside. He is monitoring their toilet-stop activities but is arrested by a policeman who suspects him of being a peeping Tom.

This scene was filmed at the public toilets on East Dulwich Road, looking onto Peckham Rye Common in East Dulwich, South London. This filming location is around four miles south-east of the South Bank Studios.

Today the public toilets remain largely unchanged as far as the building is concerned. However, as you can see from a photograph (seen in the image section of the book) taken in

December 2008, the toilets are no longer in public use. It would also seem that the site is up for let. Another noticeable change is that the surrounding undergrowth has grown somewhat since the episode was filmed there some thirty-five years earlier.

Series 7 – Closing Credits

As the closing credits roll throughout the seventh series we see a bus driving down a street lined with shops. At the end of the street is a roundabout and large entrance gates to a public park. Those same gates can be seen in the Series 7 episode 'The Allowance' as the bus turns at the roundabout.

This location can be found at the junction of Morden Road and Morden Hall Road in Morden, South-West London. The filming location was quite some distance from LWT's base at South Bank Studios, being over eight miles south-west of the studios.

My photograph of this filming location (see the image section) as it looks today show the gates as unchanged. However, whereas there was a small traffic island at the road junction when On The Buses was filmed, now a larger roundabout has taken its place. Also in the closing credits, if you look closely enough, the bus can be seen passing a Woolworths store. That store had been relocated and was nearer to the gates when I visited the site, but the store has now closed as Woolworths went into administration. Other changes include narrowing of the road and widening of the pavements to allow for a cycle path, and the trees lining the boundaries of Morden Hall Park have grown a great deal since the classic sitcom was filmed at this site.

THE FILMS

On The Buses had established itself as one of Britain's favourite sitcoms on television and had built up a huge fan base by the end of the third series in the spring of 1970. The creators Ronald Wolfe and Ronald Chesney had plotlines in mind that were just too intricate and adventurous to fit into a normal half-hour episode and so the pair were keen to take On The Buses onto the big screen. In a dramatic change of tack, London Transport wrote a letter to the creators (which was later framed and hung on their office wall) asking to be involved in the film - such was the impact that the TV series had made across the country. With backing, too, from an unlikely source in the form of Hammer Films, famed for their classic horror films, the first On The Buses film went into production.

In the summer of 1971 the film, simply called On The Buses, hit the big screen for the first time. All of the regular cast from the TV series were present and were supported by a wealth of comedy stars such as Brian Oulton, David Lodge, Pat Coombs and Wendy Richard. Even though it was made on a low budget and filmed in a matter of weeks, the film proved to be a box office smash hit. The On The Buses film was panned by the critics, but the viewing public loved it and it became the highest gross earner at the British box office in 1971, even beating the James Bond film Diamonds Are Forever to the top spot.

After such a massive success with the first film a further big-screen release was always on the cards, and less than a year later, in June 1972, the second On The Buses film was in the cinemas. The Hammer Films production was called Mutiny On The Buses and alongside the regulars were David Lodge, Bob Todd, Janet Mahoney, Pat Ashton and Kevin Brennan. Although it may not have achieved the same level of success at the box office as the first film, it remains one of Hammer's highest box-office receipt earners, and again from a low-budget film.

The TV series had run its course, with Michael Robbins leaving at the end of the sixth series and Reg Varney departing midway through the seventh and last series, but both were back on board when the third and last film premiered at Christmas 1973. Filmed on location in North Wales, the film was called Holiday On The Buses and boasted perhaps the strongest cast of the three films. As well as the regulars, the cast included Henry McGee, Wilfrid Brambell, Kate Williams, Arthur Mullard and Queenie Watts. Another decent success at the box office, Holiday On The Buses is widely regarded among the fans as their favourite film of the three.

Sadly, Holiday On The Buses brought an end to the trilogy and signalled the end of an era. The three films still receive regular television screenings and continue to introduce a new generation of fans to On The Buses. This serves as further proof, if any were needed, that the classic sitcom is indeed a comedy phenomenon.

On The Buses (1971)

Film Synopsis

It's a great life On The Buses for Stan and Jack when there is a staff shortage at the bus depot. They can break the rules, wind up Inspector Blake without fear of the sack and there is plenty of overtime available. Blakey is determined to gain the upper hand in the power struggle and his next move sees him upset the male workforce.

When the Inspector announces that he is to introduce female bus drivers to the depot it causes major problems. It not only forces Stan and Jack to pay more attention to Blakey and his rules, but it also diminishes Stan's overtime. This, in turn, encourages Olive to take on a job at the depot canteen to bring desperately needed income into the Butler household following mum's ill-timed purchase of a new washing machine.

The introduction of female drivers also has an effect on Stan's love life. He falls for Sally, one of the drivers, and when he takes things further his male colleagues take offence. As things heat up for Stan and Sally they intervene to ruin the romance.

Against the odds, Olive falls pregnant and is forced to give up her job. At the same time, Stan's overtime has dried up. As a result, Stan and Jack decide to wage a war of dirty tricks to discredit the female drivers. They use diversion signs to mislead them, put spiders in their cabs and even use diuretic tablets to cause the women more problems.

Meanwhile Stan has problems of his own, as he has an accident in his bus, wrecking a telephone box and bus shelter, and has to go through the ordeal of a test on a skidpan to prove that he is worthy of his insurance cover. It's no fun for Blakey either, as he gets a rough ride during the test.

A battle of the sexes is in full flow at the bus depot, with the men fighting for their livelihood and jobs and the women out to prove that they are up to the task. Who will win out, and will life ever be the same again at the bus depot? Time will tell.

CAST:

Stan Butler	Reg Varney
Stan's Mum	Doris Hare

Arthur, Stan's Brother-in-law	Michael Robbins
Olive, Stan's sister	Anna Karen
Inspector 'Blakey' Blake	Stephen Lewis
Jack, Stan's Conductor	Bob Grant
Betty	Andrea Lawrence
Sally	Pat Ashton
Bus Depot Manager	Brian Oulton
Ruby	Pamela Cundell
Vera	Pat Coombs
Housewife	Wendy Richard
Mr Brooks	Peter Madden
Busman	David Lodge
Bridget	Brenda Grogan
Sandra	Caroline Dowdeswell
Ada	Eunice Black
Peggy	Claire Davenport
Gladys	Maggie McGrath
Mavis	Jeanne Varney
Betty's Husband	Nosher Powell
Harry	Tex Fuller
Nobby	Terry Duggan
Eileen	Anna Michaels
London Transport Official	Norman Mitchell
First Policeman	Ivor Salter
Second Policeman	George Roderick
Motorcycle Cop	Gavin Campbell
Parson	David Rowlands
Old Woman	Hilda Barry
Suzy	Jeanette Wild
Katy	Moira Foot
Medical Orderly	Reginald Peters

WRITTEN AND PRODUCED BY: Ronald Wolfe and Ronald Chesney

DIRECTED BY:	Harry Booth
MUSIC COMPOSED BY:	Max Harris

CREW:

Production Manager	Christopher Neame
Production Supervisor	Roy Skeggs
Director of Photography	Mark McDonald
Production Designer	Scott McGregor
Film Editor	Archie Ludski GBFE
Musical Supervisor	Philip Martell
Assistant Director	Derek Whitehurst
Sound Recordist	John Purchese
Sound Editor	Peter Keen
Camera Operator	Neil Binney
Continuity	Doreen Dearnaley
Make-up Supervisor	Eddie Knight
Wardrobe Supervisor	Rosemary Burrows
Wardrobe Mistress	June Kirby
Hairdressing Supervisor	Ivy Emmerton
Assistant Art Director	Ron Benton
Construction Manager	Bill Greene
Recording Director	Tony Lumkin
Dubbing Mixer	Billy Rowe

'It's a Great Life On The Buses':

Music by	Geoff Unwin
Lyrics by	Roger Ferris
Sung by	Quinceharmon

A HAMMER PRODUCTION
Made at EMI-MGM ELSTREE STUDIOS
Hertfordshire, England

Mutiny On The Buses (1972)

Film Synopsis

Stan is all set to settle down and marry Suzy, a clippie at the depot, but he faces a number of obstacles. His family are not keen on the idea and matters are complicated when Arthur is made redundant. Olive is worried about how she will now feed her son and Stan is put under pressure to postpone the wedding.

Further problems arise for Stan at the depot when a new General Manager takes over. Mr Jenkins is determined to rule the depot with an iron rod. His plans include expansion and he orders all staff to wear proper uniforms, threatening them with the sack should they fail to comply.

Stan, who is looking for ways to raise extra cash to pay towards a flat to share with fiancée Suzy once they are married, attempts to train Arthur to drive a bus while on duty in order to secure him a job at the depot. After many hilarious incidents, which include sabotaging the company's radio control system, Stan and Jack succeed in their task and the depot employs Arthur as a bus driver.

Meanwhile, Stan and Jack continue winding up the Inspector and make an enemy of Mr Jenkins in the process. Hopes of moving into a flat are ruined by a price increase and so Stan must find a way to earn more money if he wants to get married. When the company announces that it is to start running special bus tours Suzy suggests that Stan should apply for the job of driving the bus, as the wages that go with the post are higher. The problem is that he has made an enemy of the General Manager and therefore stands no chance, and so Stan and Jack resort to a spot of blackmail.

With the job in the bag, Stan and Blakey go on a trial run to Windsor Safari Park. If Stan wants to marry Suzy everything has to go smoothly, but animal mayhem is just around the corner.

CAST:

Stan Butler	Reg Varney
Stan's Mum	Doris Hare
Arthur, Stan's Brother-in-law	Michael Robbins
Olive, Stan's sister	Anna Karen
Inspector 'Blakey' Blake	Stephen Lewis
Jack, Stan's Conductor	Bob Grant
Suzy	Janet Mahoney
Norah	Pat Ashton
Mr Jenkins, Depot General Manager	Kevin Brennan
New Inspector	Bob Todd
Safari Guard	David Lodge
Harry	Tex Fuller
Sandra	Caroline Dowdeswell
Gloria	Jan Rennison
Mrs Jenkins	Damaris Hayman
Gladys	Juliet Duncan
Pilot	Michael Nightingale
Policeman (Safari Park)	Roger Avon
Policeman (Mobile)	Barry Linehan
Policeman (On Beat)	David Rowlands
Nurse	Nicolette Chaffey
Angry Passenger	Dervis Ward
Olive's Baby	Wayne Westhorpe

WRITTEN AND PRODUCED BY:	Ronald Wolfe and Ronald Chesney
DIRECTED BY:	Harry Booth
MUSIC COMPOSED BY:	Ron Grainer
CREW:	
Musical Supervisor	Philip Martell
Production Manager	Christopher Neame
Production Supervisor	Roy Skeggs
Director of Photography	Mark McDonald BSC

Production Designer	Scott McGregor
Film Editor	Archie Ludski GBFE
Assistant Director	Ken Baker
Sound Recordist	John Purchese
Sound Editor	Roy Baker GBFE
Camera Operator	Neil Binney
Continuity	Doreen Dearnaley
Make-Up Supervisor	Eddie Knight
Wardrobe Supervisor	Dulcie Midwinter
Wardrobe Mistress	Mike Jarvis
Hairdressing Supervisor	Ivy Emmerton
Assistant Art Director	Don Picton
Construction Manager	Arthur Banks
Recording Director	Tony Lumkin
Dubbing Mixer	Bill Rowe
Gaffer	Roy Bond

A HAMMER PRODUCTION
Made at EMI-MGM Elstree Studios Hertfordshire, England

Holiday On The Buses (1973)

Film Synopsis

The inevitable finally happens when Stan and Jack are sacked after causing an accident at the bus depot. The manager is injured, two buses are written off and Inspector Blake not only injures his foot in the incident but also gets his marching orders.

When Stan and Jack land a new job working at a holiday camp in charge of a tour bus they feel sure that they have fallen on their feet. However, they are in for a shock, as they discover a familiar face in charge of camp security - none other than their old enemy, Blakey.

A change of scenery it may be, but it is just like being back at the bus depot with Blakey watching their every move.

When Stan's mum, sister and brother-in-law visit the camp on holiday this interferes with his love life plans, but there is hope for Mrs Butler in this regard when she befriends fellow holidaymaker, Bert.

Although Mrs Butler is enjoying herself, Stan finds that his romantic pursuits are constantly foiled by his nephew Arthur and two possessive mothers. While he continues to try to get a girlfriend, Arthur and Olive get into scrapes of their own, with Olive even ending up in a stranger's bed. The couple do find time to partake in dancing, but even that is destined to end in embarrassment.

Stan and Jack at last think that they have cracked it when they line up a date with two holidaymakers and take them on a mystery bus tour. However, they are destined for a night of disaster that sees them lose more than just their new girlfriends.

CAST:

Stan Butler	Reg Varney
Inspector Blake	Stephen Lewis
Mrs Mabel Butler	Doris Hare
Arthur	Michael Robbins
Olive	Anna Karen
Jack	Bob Grant
Bert Thompson	Wilfrid Brambell
Red Cross Nurse	Kate William
Wally Briggs	Arthur Mullard
Mrs Briggs	Queenie Watts
Holiday Camp Manager	Henry McGee
Little Arthur	Adam Rhodes
Depot Manager	Michael Sheard
Mrs Coombs	Hal Dyer
Luigi	Franco De Rosa
Maria	Gigi Gatti
Mrs Hudson	Eunice Black

Mavis	Maureen Sweeney
Sandra	Sandra Bryant
Doreen	Carolae Donoghue
Joyce	Tara Lynn
Patient	Alex Munro

WRITTEN AND PRODUCED BY:	Ronald Wolfe and Ronald Chesney
DIRECTED BY:	Bryan Izzard
MUSIC COMPOSED BY:	Denis King

Production Manager	Ron Jackson
Production Supervisor	Roy Skeggs
Assistant Director	Ken Baker
Musical Supervisor	Philip Martell
Director of Photography	Brian Probyn BSC
Art Director	Don Picton
Film Editor	James Needs
Choreographer	Malcolm Clare
Special Effects	Les Bowie
Sound Recordist	Claude Hitchcock
Sound Editor	Roy Hyde
Camera Operator	Rodney Anstiss
Continuity	Sally Ball
Makc-up Supcrvisor	Ricky Rickcrby
Wardrobe Supervisor	Laura Nightingale
Hairdressing Supervisor	Elaine Bowerbank
Construction Manager	Arthur Banks
Recording Director	Tony Lumkin
Dubbing Mixer	William Rowe
Gaffer	Ted Hallows

A HAMMER PRODUCTION
Made on location in Wales
and at EMI-MGM Elstree Studios, Hertfordshire England

FILM CREW
Production Team

RONALD WOLFE AND RONALD CHESNEY

On The Buses Films Produced: 3

Film Producer Career

Not only were Ronald Wolfe and Ronald Chesney the creators and writers of On The Buses, they were also on the production team and wrote all the scripts for the three films. As has already been mentioned earlier, Wolfe and Chesney put an incredible amount of work into making On The Buses such a hit and their work as producers on the three films was invaluable. It meant that the men who knew how to get the laughs on paper and knew all members of the cast's strengths could work behind the cameras to produce three films that captured the spirit of On The Buses perfectly.

As producers this was to be the only such work done by Wolfe and Chesney who were primarily scriptwriters.

FILMOGRAPHY

Film

On The Buses (1971)
Mutiny On The Buses (1972)
Holiday On The Buses (1973)

ROY SKEGGS

On The Buses Films Produced: 3

Production Supervisor Film Career

Roy Skeggs was a key part of the production team for the On The Buses trilogy. He worked as a production supervisor on all three films and his career in production was to run for over two decades.

The first On The Buses film in 1971 was Roy Skeggs' first venture into film production and he was to remain at Hammer Films for a large slice of his career. A few months after On The Buses hit the big screen Roy worked as the production supervisor on the horror film Blood from the Mummy's Tomb. This was closely followed by another Hammer Films production, also in 1971, called Dr Jekyll and Sister Hyde.

In 1972 Skeggs worked as the production supervisor on the spin-off comedy film That's Your Funeral before working on another Hammer horror production called Vampire Circus, a highly rated film. This project was soon followed by the second film in the On The Buses trilogy.

Mutiny On The Buses hit the big screen in the summer of 1972 and once more Roy was on the production team. Just a few weeks later came the latest Hammer horror film Dracula A.D. 1972, which boasted a star-studded cast that included legends Christopher Lee and Peter Cushing, and other well-known faces such as Stephanie Beacham playing supporting roles.

After two more Hammer horror films, Fear of the Night and Demons of the Mind, in 1972, Roy Skeggs returned as the production supervisor for Holiday On The Buses. This film brought a fine end to the trilogy in 1973. The end to Skeggs' career as a production supervisor came in 1974 with another Hammer film called Captain Kronos – Vampire Hunter.

Roy Skeggs was also highly accomplished as a producer, both in film and television. He split his career between comedy and horror productions, working on classic comedies such as Nearest and Dearest, Love Thy Neighbour, Man About the House, George and Mildred and Rising Damp, all in the film genre. His horror films included The Satanic Rites of Dracula and Frankenstein and the Monster from Hell. On television he produced a number of episodes of the cult series Hammer House of Horror.

Roy Skeggs went on to become Chairman at Hammer Films, but will always be remembered for his valuable contribution to the success of the three On The Buses films.

FILMOGRAPHY

Film

On The Buses (1971)
Blood from the Mummy's Tomb (1971)
Dr Jekyll and Sister Hyde (1971)
That's Your Funeral (1972)
Vampire Circus (1972)
Mutiny On The Buses (1972)
Fear in the Night (1972)
Dracula A.D. 1972 (1972)
Demons of the Mind (1972)
Holiday On The Buses (1973)
Captain Kronos – Vampire Hunter (1974)

THE DIRECTORS

HARRY BOOTH

On The Buses Films Directed: 2

Career as a Director

Harry Booth is a highly regarded figure in show business and has a wealth of experience in the industry stretching back to 1941. He has proved himself as multi-talented, having directed and produced films and television shows as well as having worked as a scriptwriter and editor.

Booth's first job in the role of director was on a 1960 war documentary called Blitz on Britain. A year later, at the end of 1961, he directed an episode of the historical TV series Sir Francis Drake, which featured a young actor destined for stardom later in life called Michael Crawford. The ITC (Incorporated Television Company) production aired on ITV and proved to be very popular.

Booth was involved with another ITC production the following year when he directed a total of five episodes of the crime series, Man of the World, in 1962 and 1963.

It was in 1965 that he directed the film documentary A King's Story. The plot followed the life story of King Edward VIII, taking us through his infancy, reign and eventual abdication in 1936. Among the cast were the Duke and Duchess of Windsor and it featured narration from the legendary actor Orson Welles. A King's Story was to have the distinction of being nominated for an Oscar for 'Best Documentary' three years later, in 1968; sadly it missed out on the accolade.

Fondly remembered today are products of the Children's Film Foundation and in 1967 Harry Booth was heavily involved in directing The Magnificent Six and ½ and River Rivals. Both of these films were also written by him and more success was on the horizon.

In 1970 came the now cult children's TV series Here Come the Double Deckers, which ran for one series and seventeen episodes from 1970 to 1971. Booth directed fourteen of those episodes and penned half a dozen of them. Here Come the Double Deckers aired on the BBC, and although unmistakably British it was a product of the massive US production company 20th Century Fox Television. The show was a lovely mix of song, dance, adventures and lots of fun based around a gang of kids who play in an abandoned double-decker bus in London.

Buses played a big part in Harry Booth's next role as director. In 1971 he was responsible for directing the original On The Buses film, which proved to be a box-office smash hit. In fact, this Hammer Films production remains that company's biggest box-office success to this day. Harry remained in the director's chair for the second part of the trilogy, Mutiny On The Buses, in 1972, although he was not involved in the third and final film. However, he was to work alongside Reg Varney again.

Late in 1972 the comedy film Go For A Take was directed by Booth. The film starred Reg Varney and Norman Rossington as two waiters on the run from crooks who are owed money. Despite a cast littered with comedy talent such as John Clive, Bill Fraser, Melvyn Hayes, David Lodge and Bob Todd, the film (co-written by Harry Booth and Alan Hackney) is not regarded as Reg's best piece of work, but it is still an enjoyable romp.

After writing and directing another Children's Film Foundation television one-off called The Flying Sorcerer in 1973, Harry directed one episode of the classic crime series The Protectors. The ITC production was a hit that ran from 1972 to 1974 and two series starring Robert Vaughn and Nyree Dawn Porter.

Harry Booth's last piece of work as a director was on an Anglo-Australian series in 1975 called Ben Hall. The programme focused on an Australian bushranger who worked as a farmer and got into scrapes with the police.

Harry Booth has continued to work in the trade, moving

on to the role of editor. He can look back on his career with great pride and satisfaction at what he has achieved in film and television production.

FILMOGRAPHY
Film
A King's Story (1965)
On The Buses (1971)
Mutiny On The Buses (1972)
Go For A Take (1972)
Going Dutch (1973)

Television
Blitz on Britain (1960)
Sir Francis Drake (1961)
Man of the World (1962-1963)
The Sentimental Agent (1963)
The Magnificent Six and ½ (1967)
River Rivals (1967)
Here Come the Double Deckers (1970-1971)
Bachelor of Arts (1971)
The Pathfinders (1972)
The Flying Sorcerer (1973)
The Protectors (1973)
Ben Hall (1975)

BRYAN IZZARD

On The Buses Films Directed: 1

Career as a Director
Bryan Izzard was one of the most prolific directors of the 1970s and was a renowned producer too. It was with London Weekend Television in 1971 that he directed his first television show, sharing the directing role on the children's fantasy series Jamie. It followed the adventures of a young boy who discovers a magic carpet that allows him to travel

through time.

Also in 1971 the spin-off sitcom The Fenn Street Gang began and it was to prove successful. Izzard directed the LWT show for twenty-six of its forty-seven episodes from 1971 to 1973 and he was also on the production team for a handful of episodes.

Another hit sitcom to be directed by Bryan Izzard, again an LWT production, was Doctor in Charge. The medical sitcom ran for forty-three episodes and two series from 1972 to 1973 and Izzard was part of a five-man directing team that worked on the programme.

After having directed and produced a number of episodes of On The Buses in 1972 and 1973, Bryan Izzard was handed the task of directing the film Holiday On The Buses in 1973. This was his first shot at film directing and he made a very fine job of it, as the film remains a favourite of the fans.

The short-lived but highly rated sitcom Not on Your Nellie was Izzard's next project. He produced and directed all seventeen episodes over three series from 1974 to 1975. Hylda Baker took the starring role and it included appearances from Michael Sheard and Wendy Richard (both of whom had parts in On The Buses), among others.

There was to be a change for Izzard with his next project, as he ventured into drama. He directed five episodes, spread over three years from 1972 to 1974, of the classic courtroom drama Crown Court. This Granada TV production went on to become one of the longest-running dramas on British television, extending over twelve years from 1972 to 1984.

A much-forgotten but highly rated sitcom called The Top Secret Life of Edgar Briggs hit the TV screens in autumn 1974. Izzard shared the directing duties with Bruce Gowers, and David Jason starred in one of his early sitcom appearances. The comedy ran for just one thirteen-episode series.

Another successful sitcom directed by Izzard came in the form of the spin-off Doctor on the Go, starring Robin Nedwell, Geoffrey Davies and Ernest Clark. He directed all twenty-six episodes of this sitcom, which ran from 1975 to 1977, alongside Gerry Mill and Alan Wallis.

Bryan's next assignment was to direct half a dozen episodes of the classic prison drama Within These Walls, starring Googie Withers. His work on the show came in 1975 and 1976. A few months later he got the chance to work on another Wolfe and Chesney-scripted sitcom, but it was a brief association as he directed just one episode of The Rag Trade in 1977.

Izzard remained active in the television production trade, but his next notable piece of work did not come until 1991. It was a rarity, too, as the show was a BBC production and the majority of his work had been for LWT. The underrated sitcom An Actor's Life for Me ran for a mere six episodes, all directed by Izzard, and starred John Gordon Sinclair and Victor Spinetti.

Bryan's final project was his role as director of a film called Julie and the Cadillacs in 1999. The plot was about a struggling pop group in the 1960s lured to London. Sadly, the film was not destined to be a success and was a low-key way for Izzard to end his career as a director.

Sadly, on 27th April 2006, at his home in Surrey, Bryan Izzard passed away at the age of seventy-four. His career record as a producer and director speaks for itself. He was one of the most prolific directors of his generation and is sadly missed.

FILMOGRAPHY

Film

Holiday On The Buses (1973)
Julie and the Cadillacs (1999)

Television

Jamie (1971)
The Fenn Street Gang (1971-1973)
On The Buses (1972-1973)
Doctor in Charge (1972-1973)
New Scotland Yard (1972)
Crown Court (1972-1974)
The Reg Varney Revue (1972)
Not on Your Nellie (1974-1975)

The Top Secret Life of Edgar Briggs (1974)
Within These Walls (1975-1976)
Doctor on the Go (1975-1977)
The Rag Trade (1977)
Rep (1982)
Here's a Funny Thing (1982)
Interference (1983)
Red Peppers (1991)
An Actor's Life for Me (1991)

THE COMPOSERS

MAX HARRIS

On The Buses Film Soundtracks: 1

Career as a Composer

Max Harris was not only a noted composer but also a pianist and bandleader. He composed themes for a number of classic television series and films in a career that was to span over thirty years.

After almost a decade in the art of composing Harris took on the role of arranging and blending the catchy theme tune 'It's a Great Life On The Buses' into various scenes of the On The Buses film in 1971. Although Max Harris's name appears in the credits, it must be said that the song itself was composed by the talented Geoff Unwin, with the lyrics supplied by Roger Ferris. The largely unknown band Quinceharmon performed the song, which set the mood quite superbly for the film.

Harris is also responsible for composing the theme for the much-maligned Carry On England film in 1976. In addition, the classic sitcoms Porridge, Mind Your Language and Open All Hours all boasted theme tunes composed by Max Harris.

Sadly, Max Harris is no longer with us, having passed away on 13th March 2004 at the age of eighty-five, but his music legacy lives on.

FILMOGRAPHY

Film

Baby Love (1968)

On The Buses (1971)

Carry on England (1976)

Television

The Strange World of Gurney Slade (1960)
Drama 61-67 (1961-1967)
Sherlock Holmes (1964-1968)
Hit and Run (1965)
Barney is My Darling (1965)
The Wednesday Play (1966-1967)
Thirty-Minute Theatre (1967)
The Intrepid Mr Twigg (1968)
The Gold Robbers (1969)
Wink to Me Only (1969)
Doomwatch (1970)
Seven of One (1973)
Casanova '73 (1973)
Porridge (1974-1977)
Carry On Laughing (1975)
Open All Hours (1976-1985)
Mind Your Language (1977-1986)
A Horseman Riding By (1978)
Here's a Funny Thing (1982)
What a Carry On (1983-1984)
A Gentleman's Club (1988)
The Christmas Wife (1988)
Blackeyes (1989)

RON GRAINER

On The Buses Film Soundtracks: 1

Career as a Composer

The Australian composer Ron Grainer is responsible for some of the most memorable television theme tunes of all time. His work over twenty years in the British film and television industry saw him win several awards, and to this day, many years after his death, his music is still in use on British television.

Grainer was to compose the toe-tapping instrumental

music heard throughout Mutiny On The Buses. The score, much like that of the original, does a great job of capturing the mood of the film. The theme was later released on an album called 'The Hammer Comedy Film Music Collection'.

Perhaps Ron will be best remembered for the classic theme that he composed for the long-running BBC sci-fi series Doctor Who. However, he won successive Ivor Novello Awards in 1961 and 1962 for his composition of the theme to the BBC detective series Maigret in 1960, which was later released as a single by Joe Loss and his Orchestra and reached number 20 in the UK charts in 1962. Grainer's other award came in 1962 for a tune called 'Old Ned', which is better known as the theme of the classic BBC sitcom Steptoe and Son.

In 1967 Grainer composed the memorable theme to the ITC detective series Man in a Suitcase and was also responsible for the score for the cult series The Prisoner, which first aired that year, as well as writing the soundtrack for the 1967 hit film To Sir, With Love.

Through into the 1970s Grainer continued producing memorable film and television scores. In 1971 he wrote the music for the Charlton Heston film The Omega Man and was also involved in composing for television, such as the theme of For the Love of Ada. The classic haunting theme of Tales of the Unexpected was another to be composed by him in 1979 and he also wrote the theme music for the popular Thames Television comedy Shelley in the same year.

Tragically, on 21st February 1981, at the age of just fifty-eight, Ron Grainer lost his battle against cancer of the spine and died in Cuckfield Hospital in Surrey. Thanks to the continued success of Doctor Who, Ron's work can still be heard fronting hit TV series today, over a quarter of a century after his death. This is a testament to the sheer quality of the musical scores that he wrote.

FILMOGRAPHY

Film

We Joined the Navy (1962)
A Kind of Loving (1962)

Some People (1962)
Live Now – Pay Later (1962)
The Dock Brief (1962)
Station Six – Sahara (1962)
The Mouse on the Moon (1963)
The Caretaker (1963)
The Running Man (1963)
Nothing But the Best (1964)
Night Must Fall (1964)
The Moon Spinners (1964)
The Finest Hours (1964)
To Sir, With Love (1967)
Only When I Larf (1968)
The Assassination Bureau (1969)
Before Winter Comes (1969)
Lock Up Your Daughters (1969)
In Search of Gregory (1969)
Hoffman (1970)
The Omega Man (1971)
Mutiny On The Buses (1972)
Steptoe and Son (1972)
Yellow Dog (1973)
Steptoe and Son Ride Again (1973)
One Way (1976)
I Don't Want to Be Born (1976)
The Bawdy Adventures of Tom Jones (1976)
Never Never Land (1980)

Television
ITV Television Playhouse (1959-1960)
The Men from Room 13 (1959)
ITV Play of the Week (1960)
Maigret (1960-1961)
Terminus (1961)
It's a Square World (1961-1964)
That Was the Week That Was (1962-1963)
Steptoe and Son (1962-1974)
Oliver Twist (1962)

The Six Proud Walkers (1962)
The Old Curiosity Shop (1962-1963)
Comedy Playhouse (1963-1964)
The King's Breakfast (1963)
Doctor Who (1963-)
Not So Much of a Programme, More of a Way of Life (1964-1965)
The Flying Swan (1965)
Disneyland (1966)
All Gas and Gaiters (1966-1971)
Uncle Charles (1967)
Blandings Castle (1967)
The Reluctant Romeo (1967)
The Old Campaigner (1967)
Boy Meets Girl (1967)
The Prisoner (1967-1968)
Man in a Suitcase (1967-1968)
The Wednesday Play (1967-1969)
The Jazz Age (1968)
Play of the Month (1969)
Destiny of a Spy (1969)
For the Love of Ada (1970-1971)
Paul Temple (1971)
The Trouble with Lilian (1971)
Thief (1971)
The Train Now Standing (1972-1973)
And No One Could Save Her (1973)
Mousey (1974)
South Riding (1974)
Kim & Co. (1975)
Romance (1977)
Armchair Thriller (1978)
Born and Bred (1978-1980)
Edward and Mrs Simpson (1978)
Rebecca (1979)
Malice Aforethought (1979)
Tales of the Unexpected (1979-1982)
Shelley (1979-1983)
A Question of Guilt (1980)

ITV Playhouse (1980)
It Takes a Worried Man (1981-1983)
Saturday Night Thriller (1982)

DENIS KING

On The Buses Film Soundtracks: 1

Career as a Composer

Denis King was to compose the music for the Holiday On The Buses film and, much like Max Harris and Ron Grainer, he is responsible for writing many classic theme tunes for film and television. His work in the industry spans over three decades, and although he has not been as prolific as Ron Grainer his career record is still very impressive.

It was in 1973 that King composed the theme for the third part of the On The Buses film trilogy. The score, although not as up-tempo as the previous films, is a jolly soundtrack that certainly fits the bill as far as themes go. King also composed the other scores heard throughout the Holiday On The Buses film.

Denis King's most noted work came in the 1970s when he composed 'Galloping Home' – a powerful and memorable score used to front the children's classic series The Adventures of Black Beauty. The series ran from 1972 to 1974, and when it was resurrected many years later, in 1992 for Australian television, Denis King's score was used once more. The haunting and atmospheric theme of the adventure series Dick Turpin is another famous piece of music that was composed by King in the late 1970s. He was also the man behind the theme tunes for the sitcoms The Fosters and Not on Your Nellie as well as the children's favourite Worzel Gummidge.

Into the 1980s King continued to write numerous scores used in film and on television. The theme for the BBC drama Lovejoy was courtesy of King and the quality spy drama Hannay also benefited from one of his scores.

There is no doubt that Denis King is one of the best contributors of scores on British television and his work has stood the test of time. He will also be remembered for playing his part in setting the mood for the On The Buses films, much like Max Harris, Geoff Unwin and Ron Grainer before him.

FILMOGRAPHY

Film

Simon, Simon (1970)
Not Tonight, Darling (1971)
The Chairman's Wife (1971)
The Spy's Wife (1972)
Foursome (1972)
Ghost in the Noonday Sun (1973)
Holiday On The Buses (1973)
Footsteps (1974)
Sweeney (1977)
Son of Hitler (1978)
Privates on Parade (1982)
Sista dansen (1993)

Television

Comedy Playhouse (1971)
The Adventures of Black Beauty (1972-1974)
Between the Wars (1973)
Within These Walls (1974-1976)
Not on Your Nellie (1974-1975)
The Fosters (1976-1977)
Holding On (1977)
Armchair Thriller (1978)
Dick Turpin (1979-1982)
How's Your Father (1979)
Worzel Gummidge (1979-1981)
Holding the Fort (1980-1981)
Rhubarb Rhubarb (1980)
Smuggler (1981)
If You Go Down in the Woods Today (1981)
Now and Then (1983-1984)

Minder (1985)
Lovejoy (1986-1994)
The Worst Witch (1986)
The Fools on the Hill (1986)
Ffizz (1987-1989)
Hannay (1988-1989)
The New Adventures of Black Beauty (1990)
Moon and Son (1992)
Heavy Weather (1995)
Madson (1996)
Out of Sight (1997-1999)

FILMING LOCATIONS

The Films

All three spin-off films were filmed at the EMI-MGM Elstree Studios in Borehamwood, Hertfordshire. This meant that, unlike the television series which were filmed in London, the filming locations would be found in close proximity to the studios on the streets of Borehamwood and the nearby village of Shenley, which is just a couple of miles to the north-east. However, each of the three films did have at least one scene shot away from the Borehamwood area, as will be revealed later.

In 1971 came the first On The Buses film, which was to use a number of filming locations in Borehamwood and less so in nearby Shenley. The scene where Stan is forced to undergo a test after an accident and has to drive the bus on a skidpan was filmed at London Transport's facility in Chiswick, West London, which unfortunately closed in 1983 and the site has since been redeveloped.

Mutiny On The Buses was also filmed largely in Borehamwood, incorporating locations used in the first film as well as new sites. Shenley was once more chosen as an ideal filming location for certain scenes owing to the quiet, secluded nature of the area. Up until that point, all television and film locations used in On The Buses had been within close proximity to the studios, but Mutiny On The Buses was to buck that trend in 1972 when scenes were shot on location at Windsor Safari Park, meaning a trip of almost forty miles to the south-west of the studios for the cast, crew and equipment. Sadly, Windsor Safari Park finally closed for business in 1992.

The final spin-off film Holiday On The Buses (1973) was to venture even further afield for location shots. Aside from the opening scenes of the film, which were filmed in Borehamwood, the film was shot entirely on location in North Wales, the main site being the holiday camp run by Pontins in the seaside town of Prestatyn, although a number of other filming locations were used in the surrounding Welsh resorts and countryside.

The pick of the filming locations from the three films will now be revealed, with photographs to be found in the image section in the centre of the book showing the locations as they look today.

The Bus Depot

In all three spin-off films we can see exterior shots of buses entering and exiting the bus depot, as well as Olive entering the depot aboard Arthur's motorbike and sidecar. It is also seen at the start of Holiday On The Buses when Stan has an accident, crashing his bus as he exits the depot while ogling a young woman.

The building masquerading as the bus depot was none other than Stage 5 at the EMI-MGM Elstree Studios in Borehamwood. This was the same stage where a number of smash hit films including Star Wars were filmed, as well as the hit children's television series Here Come the Double Deckers. Sadly, however, the stage and other portions of the famous studios have since disappeared and made way for redevelopment.

It was in 1991 that Stage 5 was demolished. The site is now occupied by a large Tesco supermarket, car park and petrol station (as seen in the photograph in the image section). Aptly enough, a number of buses now use part of the site as either a terminus or bus stop.

The Butler Residence

We see several exterior shots of the Butler house, chiefly in the first two spin-off films but also briefly in Holiday On The Buses. The house is first seen in the opening credits sequence of the On The Buses film. We see the exterior of the house again in Mutiny On The Buses when Olive is mounting the motorbike as she prepares to go to the bus depot to check up on Arthur, as she believes he is seeing another woman. In Holiday On The Buses the Butler house exterior is seen again when the family are preparing to depart for the holiday camp.

The Butler house in the films is located in central Borehamwood at 2, Malden Road, less than half a mile away from the Elstree Film Studios (formerly EMI-MGM Elstree Studios). Within viewing distance to the right of the property is within viewing distance is the famous set for the hit soap EastEnders.

As you can see from a photograph (which can be found in the image section in the centre pages) taken recently of the filming location, the house remains much the same. The main differences are that the red-bricked garden wall has been removed, the brickwork is now cream in colour and a satellite dish has been fixed to the front of the house. Also, to the right of the house as we look at it, a new property has been built, replacing a six-foot-high fence and a street sign that were in situ when the films were shot there.

The Launderette

One of the best-loved and memorable scenes from the three spin-off films came in On The Buses, the original film in 1971. We see Stan rushing out of a launderette with what he thinks is his mum's laundry and he is caught by a waiting Inspector Blake, who takes the laundry bag from him. Two housewives (played by Wendy Richard and the late Reg Varney's daughter, Jeanne Varney) come rushing out of the launderette and set about the Inspector, accusing him of stealing their washing. A policeman is quickly on scene to hear poor Blakey being accused of being a 'knicker snatcher'.

The scene was filmed at 120, Manor Way in Borehamwood. This filming location was just over a mile to the south-east of the studios and was also used in a couple of lesser scenes of the spin-off films.

A photograph (as seen in the image section) of the location taken recently show that the launderette is still in business some thirty-eight years on. Although the signs above have changed (now called Manor Laundry and Dry Cleaner Centre), the shop remains very much the same. The road directly outside has been narrowed, but opposite the row of shops the flats seen briefly in the film remain unchanged.

Turnaround Betty's House

Another much-loved scene from the first spin-off film shows Stan almost caught in Turnaround Betty's house by her husband. He manages to get away only to demolish a bus shelter in his desperation to make a quick exit. The location is seen in other scenes throughout the film, such as when Jack emerges from the house in the process of getting dressed, with Blakey waiting outside for an explanation.

These scenes were filmed at 20, Whitehouse Avenue in

Borehamwood. This is located no more than a quarter of a mile to the south-west of the studios, and although it is a narrow street its quiet neighbourhood would have made it an ideal filming location.

Today (as seen in the photograph in the image section in the centre pages) the house remains much the same aside from a new door and windows and cream-coloured paint on the brickwork. The low wall seen outside the house in the film has gone and the small lawn has been dug up and cemented over. These are the only changes to the property and even the famous washing line is still present.

Opening Credits Sequence

During the opening credits sequence of On The Buses we see Stan's bus race past a bus stop at which a queue of people are waiting. The bus comes to a halt where Stan's mum is waiting outside a row of shops and we see Arthur standing outside a grocery shop and opening the door for Olive, who comes out holding a bagful of shopping. By the time the family have boarded the bus the people who had been queuing at the bus stop have run along the street and almost reach the bus before it leaves without them, much to their disgust.

This filming location has only been discovered in the past year and it has now been confirmed that the row of shops is situated in Rossington Avenue, Borehamwood, just under a mile-and-a-half to the north-west of the studios.

In terms of the surrounding houses and street layout, very little has changed at this filming location (as can be seen in the photograph in the image section). The pavement has seen its paving slabs replaced by a layer of tarmac and some of the shopfronts are adorned by satellite dishes. It is belief that the shop which Olive appears is now a hairdressing salon.

The Runaway Sidecar

In the first spin-off film we see Stan and Arthur aboard the motorcycle with a pregnant Olive in the sidecar. While they are en route for her check-up at the hospital she begins to go into labour, and in a rush to get to their destination we see the motorcycle airborne as it speeds over a hump-backed bridge. Then, on taking a tight turn, the sidecar splits from the motorcycle and can be seen running into a grass verge on a quiet country lane with a farm in the background.

This filming location can be found on Mimms Lane in the village of Shenley to the north-east of Borehamwood. It was just three-and-a-half miles away from the studios and in very close proximity to another filming location used in Mutiny On The Buses.

As you can see from the photograph of the location (which can be found in the image section) as it looks today, there are a few subtle differences. When the sidecar comes to rest in the film we see a different fence to the one that exists today and now a hedge and trees run along behind that fence. The building a few yards down the lane has been renovated somewhat, and trees and hedges have grown on the other side of the lane, giving it a more enclosed feeling.

Arthur's Driving Lessons

A particular location is seen on a number of occasions in Mutiny On The Buses when Stan is giving Arthur driving lessons. In one of the scenes Arthur knocks over the bus stop, and later in the film we see Stan and Jack playing darts with a dartboard perched on the bonnet when Inspector Blake arrives in his new company car.

I can now reveal that this filming location is in Rectory Lane in the village of Shenley on the outskirts of

Borehamwood and to the north-east of the studios. The location would have meant a journey of almost three-and-a-half miles for the cast, crew and equipment. Just a hundred yards further down the lane is the location of the runaway sidecar scene.

A photograph taken of the filming location as it looks today which can be seen in the image section shows very little has changed in this quiet country lane location. A wooden building seen to the left of the bus stop has been demolished and replaced by a house. The lawn on which the bus shelter (a temporary structure for filming) was situated remains, as do the trees and hedges, although they have of course grown somewhat.

Olive and the Manhole Cover

A couple of scenes from Mutiny On The Buses were filmed at our next location. In one scene Stan's bus is used to tow Arthur and Olive aboard the motorbike and sidecar after its starter breaks off. We first see the bus going uphill and it is then that the motorbike's handlebars snap off. Then the bus veers onto a side road and the motorbike combination gathers speed as it hurtles down the other side of the hill, totally out of control. The combination careers into a workman's tent in the middle of the road before continuing down the road enveloped inside the tent, leaving behind Olive who is stuck in a manhole.

Later in the film, at the same location, we see a bus with Inspector Blake aboard and driver Stan is struggling to remove a dartboard that is perched on the bonnet. He drops the dartboard and it rolls downhill and into an open manhole cover, hitting a workman on the head.

Both of these scenes were filmed on Bullhead Road in Borehamwood, which is situated just half a mile to the east of the studios.

The road used for these filming locations remains much as it was in the early 1970s (as can be seen in the photograph in the centre pages). When I visited Borehamwood to identify certain locations the instantly recognisable Oaklands College building at the foot of Bullhead Road, which can be seen clearly in the films, told me that this was indeed the site used for filming these scenes. The manhole cover remains to this day, and as for the side street down which the bus turns when the combination handlebars become detached it is my belief that this was Hillside Avenue.

Holiday Camp Gates

In the final spin-off film Holiday On The Buses we see Stan and Jack set off on their first trip aboard the holiday camp's tour bus to pick up holidaymakers from the train station. When they reach the camp gates they find them closed, and it is then that they discover that the new head of camp security is none other than their old nemesis, Blakey. The gates are seen again when the family arrive on the motorbike and sidecar to be met by Stan and Blakey at the gates.

These scenes were filmed on location and the gates are situated at the entrance to the Pontins Holiday Park in Prestatyn, North Wales. For the cast and film crew, together with their equipment, filming here meant a trip of over two-hundred-and-twenty miles to the north-west of their base at EMI-MGM Elstree Studios.

A recent trip to the Pontins Prestatyn Holiday Park enabled me to photograph this filming location. As you can see from the photograph in the image section of the book, very little has changed apart from the fact that the gates have now been painted black and the lanterns on top of the stone pillars are of a different design. Also a barrier, operated by Park Security, has now been built across the road. Running alongside the road and marking the perimeter of the camp is a hedge rather than the wooden fence seen in the film. The office from which Blakey emerges in the film remains unchanged to this day.

The Lost Luggage

A scene in Holiday On The Buses sees Arthur, Olive, Little Arthur and Mrs Butler aboard the motorbike and sidecar en route to the holiday camp. We see Stan's bus overtake the bike as it crosses a bridge, but the bus is forced to swerve to avoid an oncoming car and in turn forces the combination into a barrier. On impact, two suitcases tied to the sidecar are launched over the barrier and into the river below. Arthur and Olive can then be seen venturing into the river in a bid to retrieve their luggage. The location is also seen towards the end of the film when the motorbike combo has a similar accident while travelling home from the camp.

The two scenes were filmed on Rhuddlan Bridge in the town of Rhuddlan, Denbighshire, North Wales. This location was a mere four-and-a-half miles to the south-west of the Pontins Holiday Park in Prestatyn where the majority of the film was shot.

The filming location today remains the same, as can be seen in the photograph (see the image section) taken recently of the site, apart from a crash barrier that has now been erected on both sides of the west end of the bridge. The shots of Arthur and Olive attempting to save their suitcases were filmed on the west bank of the River Clwyd, and the riverbank does appear to have become more of a grassy verge rather than the rocky terrain seen in the film.

The Mystery Tour Stop

During the mystery tour scene in Holiday On The Buses we see the open-top bus stop at a beauty spot and a waterfall can be seen in the background. Stan has a date lined up when he finishes his shift, but he faces a race against time to make it and can be seen urging the holidaymakers on his tour, who were busy enjoying their refreshments at the time, to get back on the bus. Olive is also rushed onto the bus as she exits a shop holding a big stick of candy floss.

This filming location is Dyserth Falls in the village of Dyserth, Denbighshire, North Wales. It is situated just under three-and-a-half miles to the south-west of Pontins Holiday Park in Prestatyn and proved an ideal filming location due to its proximity to Prestatyn and its quiet, secluded surroundings.

Today the Dyserth Falls location is instantly recognisable from the shots in the film (as can be seen in the photographs in the centre pages). The grass lawn still remains but the small tables and parasols seen in the film have been replaced, as have the park benches. Aside from the planting of a new palm tree, the surrounding vegetation is unchanged and the two distinctive houses on the hill in the background remain as they were all those years ago. As for the shop from which Olive appears, it looks much the same but is currently between owners and is closed for business.

The Mystery Tour Bridge

In Holiday On The Buses Stan and Jack's mystery bus tour for the holidaymakers takes them through a seaside town and along a seafront before we see it crossing a bridge with boats moored to the right.

From the brief glimpse of the bridge that is shown in the film, the location has been identified as the North Wales seaside town of Rhyl. The bridge spans the River Clwyd at Foryd Harbour, which sits at the estuary to the Irish Sea, and it lies about five miles to the west of Pontins Holiday Park in Prestatyn.

My photograph of this filming location as it looks today (which can be seen in the image section) show the bridge to be unchanged, apart from the colour. In the film the bridge was painted grey, as were the railings running alongside it, but now, after probably countless coats of paint since 1973, it is a bright blue colour. The surrounding area is also much the same, aside from the building of new houses on the west bank of the River Clwyd.

SUPPORTING CAST
The Complete A-Z

A

ASHTON, Marcia

Marcia Ashton was born in Sheffield, Yorkshire, in 1932. Her solitary role in On The Buses came in the Series 6 episode called 'Union Trouble'. She played Elsie, who was a canteen employee set to lose her job, but Stan goes on a one-man strike in an attempt to help her remain in her post.

In an acting career that stretches over half a century Marcia has appeared in single episodes of classic television series such as Z Cars, Father, Dear Father, Upstairs Downstairs, Rumpole of the Bailey and Spooks. She has also had larger roles in the hit soaps Brookside (1992-1996) and EastEnders (2002-2003) as well as parts in the medical dramas Doctors and Holby City. She is still active in the acting trade to the present day.

ASHTON, Pat

Born in 1946, actress Pat Ashton had four sizeable roles in On The Buses. In 1971 she appeared as insatiable clippie Doreen in two Series 5 episodes, 'Stan's Room' and 'The Injury'. Also, in the same year, in the original On The Buses film she played bus driver Sally, who was the subject of Stan's amorous advances. Her final role in the classic comedy came in 1972 when she played the memorable character known as

'Nymphy Norah' in the second spin-off film Mutiny On The Buses.

Pat's television career started with her appearance as a 'Hill's Angel' on the hit comedy The Benny Hill Show. She was primarily a comedy actress and appeared in a string of sitcoms such as Romany Jones, Don't Drink the Water, Yus My Dear, The Fosters, Only When I Laugh and Tripper's Day. She also claimed another feather for her cap when she played a small role in the smash hit musical film Half a Sixpence, as well as appearing in classic dramas such as Crown Court, Dixon of Dock Green, Z Cars and Minder.

Her acting career ground to a halt in the mid-1980s after twenty years in the trade, but she is still fondly remembered for her roles in On The Buses.

AVON, Roger

Roger Avon was born in Jarrow, County Durham, in 1914 and appeared in one episode of On The Buses as well as the Mutiny On The Buses film. In the Series 4 episode 'Christmas Duty' he played the policeman who greets the Butlers when they return to the house to find that there has been a fire, and in the film he adopts the same role and is seen looking shocked as he opens the doors of the tour bus only to find a chimpanzee at the steering wheel.

Avon also appeared as a policeman in a number of other shows, including Dr Findlay's Casebook, Randall and Hopkirk (Deceased), Steptoe and Son, Softly, Softly and Yus My Dear. He also had small roles in the films Daleks Invasion Earth: 2150 A.D, Quatermass and the Pit and The Likely Lads.

Roger Avon passed away at the age of eighty-four in 1998.

B

BAPTISTE, Austin

Austin Baptiste made a brief appearance in one episode of On The Buses. In the Series 3 episode 'The Snake' he adopted the role of a musician playing an Indian set of drums as Fatima performed her snake dance.

His acting career never really took off and his only other credits came in a Canadian television series called R.C.M.P. (Royal Canadian Mounted Police) and two appearances in the ATV adventure series Virgin of the Secret Service in 1968. Austin Baptiste passed away recently.

BARRY, Hilda

Hilda Barry, born in Edmonton, London, in 1885, made her single On The Buses appearance in the 1971 spin-off film. She played the part of an old woman who tells Blakey: "I only wanted to go to Tesco's" after her bus journey overruns due to a diversion onto the motorway.

Hilda's career in show business was extensive across the genres. Dramatic television roles in Quatermass II, The Railway Children, The Edgar Wallace Mystery Theatre, The Prisoner and Z Cars, to name but a few, were intermingled with numerous roles in comedy classics such as Hancock, Steptoe and Son, Father, Dear Father and Whatever Happened To The Likely Lads? and films such as Carry On Loving and Steptoe and Son Ride Again.

Hilda Barry passed away in 1979 at the grand old age of ninety-four.

BAYNTUN, Amelia

Born in 1919, Amelia Bayntun appeared in the Series 5

episode 'Lost Property'. She played the part of the passenger on Stan's bus that reports her lost fish and chips to Inspector Blake.

Although a very active stage actress she also appeared regularly on television in the 1960s in such programmes as Dixon of Dock Green, The Wednesday Play, David Copperfield and Z Cars, her biggest role being in two series of the Thames Television sitcom Dear Mother...Love Albert. Bayntun's film career also boasted uncredited roles in the James Bond film Thunderball and the children's classic The Railway Children. She will probably be best remembered for her role as Mrs Fussy in the comedy classic film Carry On Camping and she went on to appear in Carry On Loving, Carry On at Your Convenience, Carry On Matron and Carry On Abroad.

Amelia Bayntun passed away in 1988 at the age of sixty-eight.

BIRCH, Samantha

Samantha Birch appeared briefly in one episode of On The Buses. Towards the end of the Series 4 episode called 'The Lodger' she is revealed by the Inspector to be the Assistant Traffic Manager and Stan has missed out on a chance to make her a lodger at the Butler house.

Samantha's career in show business saw her roles restricted to television and she appeared in episodes of hit sitcoms such as Doctor in the House, Hark at Barker and Doctor in Charge. She took a break from acting in the mid-1970s but returned to appear in the hit drama Doctors and has recently had a small role in a new US film called Street Boss.

BLACK, Eunice

Eunice Black, born in London in 1915, was one of the most regularly used supporting cast members in On The Buses. She appeared in four episodes in the roles of a traffic warden in 'Mum's Last Fling' (Series 3), a clippie called Rosie in 'Dangerous Driving' and 'Christmas Duty' (both Series 4) and as a clippie called Gladys in 'No Smoke Without Fire' (Series 6). She also appeared in two of the spin-off films, playing one of the butch clippies, Ada, in On The Buses (1971) and domineering mother Mrs Hudson in Holiday On The Buses (1973).

Prior to her acting career Eunice was an English and Drama teacher. She became a familiar face on British television, appearing in classic sitcoms such as Please Sir!, The Liver Birds, Doctor at Large and George and Mildred as well as The Benny Hill Show and Last of the Summer Wine.

Sadly, Eunice Black passed away in 2007 at the age of ninety-two.

BRADY, Pete

Born in Montreal, Canada, in 1942, Pete Brady's voice was heard over Olive's radio in the Series 3 episode 'Foggy Night', as a disc jockey reporting the bad fog.

In reality Pete Brady was a disc jockey with the then highly popular Radio Luxembourg. His only other venture into the media of television came when he presented the hit ITV children's show Magpie from 1968 to 1972.

BRAEMAR, Winifred

Winifred Braemar appeared in Series 4 of On The Buses as Winnie, a member of staff in the depot's canteen, in three episodes called 'The Kids Outing', 'The Lodger' and 'Not

Tonight'.

She appeared in a string of other hit sitcoms during her acting career such as Please Sir!, Doctor in the House and For the Love of Ada. Her film roles included the spin-off film of For the Love of Ada and the sex comedy Confessions from a Holiday Camp, which was her last role in film and television.

BRAMBELL, Wilfrid

Wilfrid Brambell was born in Dublin, Ireland, in 1912. He had a sizeable role in the third spin-off film Holiday On The Buses, playing holidaymaker Bert Thompson who takes a fancy to Stan's mum, Mabel Butler.

Although he went on to be remembered for his comedy roles, Brambell began his acting career in drama films such as Odd Man Out, Eyes That Kill and The 39 Steps (all uncredited) as well as television dramas such as The Quatermass Experiment, BBC Sunday Night Theatre and The Adventures of Robin Hood.

Of course he will be best remembered as rag-and-bone man Albert Steptoe in the classic sitcom Steptoe and Son (1962-1974) and its two spin-off films. He also appeared as Mr Pullen in Carry On Again Doctor and other hit comedy films such as Dry Rot, Crooks in Cloisters and What a Whopper. On television he appeared in other sitcoms such as According to Dora, Never Say Die and Citizen Smith.

It was early in 1985 that Wilfrid Brambell lost his battle against cancer and died at the age of seventy-two.

BRECK, Julia

Born in 1941 on the Isle of Wight, Julia Breck appeared in the final episode of Series 6 of On The Buses called 'The Prize', playing the part of a canteen employee at the bus depot.

Her acting career revolved around comedy roles, appearing in the controversial sitcom Curry and Chips as well as The Liver Birds, Some Mothers Do 'Ave 'Em, Monty Python's Flying Circus and sketch show The Two Ronnies. She was a member of Spike Milligan's supporting cast for his long-running comedy series called Q5.

Julia Breck retired from acting in the early 1980s and now lives in France with her husband.

BREE, James

James Bree made one solitary appearance in On The Buses in the Series 5 episode 'The Strain', playing Doctor Clark who visits Stan following a back injury sustained at work and advises him to wear a corset to protect his back from further strains.

During his lengthy acting career he appeared in a wide range of classic television shows including Z Cars, The Avengers, The Prisoner, Doctor Who (1969-1986), Randall and Hopkirk (Deceased), Upstairs Downstairs, The Persuaders, The Sweeney, The Professionals and The Jewel in the Crown. He also appeared in the James Bond film On Her Majesty's Secret Service and hit sitcoms George and the Dragon, Doctor at Large, Please Sir!, Nearest and Dearest and Rising Damp.

BREEZE, Olivia

In the Series 4 episode 'The 'L' Bus', Olivia Breeze played the part of clippie Janet, who is one of four being trained by Stan and Jack and ends up using the bus as a removal van.

Her career in show business is one that has seen her largely concentrate on stage work. Her rare television roles came in the 1970s sitcoms Charley's Grants, Doctor at Large and Maggie and Her. Olivia Breeze now works on stage as an actor, director and presenter of a range of stage shows.

BRENNAN, Kevin

Born in Australia in 1920, Kevin Brennan had a large role in Mutiny On The Buses in 1972, playing the bus depot's new manager Mr Jenkins, who is determined to rule with authority and not only makes life tough for Stan and Jack but also for Inspector Blake.

His acting career has embraced many dramatic roles on both the small and big screen. He has appeared in classic films such as Get Carter and his television roles include parts in Maigret, The Saint, The Avengers, Softly, Softly, Budgie, Z Cars, Colditz and The Professionals. Brennan is also adept in comedy roles, which have included appearances in Romany Jones, Bless This House and In Loving Memory.

BRIGGS, Johnny

Johnny Briggs was born in London in 1935 and appeared in the Series 6 episode of On The Buses called 'Love is What You Make It', playing a window cleaner who calls at the Butlers house and is mistakenly chatted up by Olive.

His acting career spans over sixty years and he had a number of small film roles in the 1960s including The Bulldog Breed, A Stitch in Time, 633 Squadron, Doctor in Distress, The Intelligence Men and Carry On Up the Khyber. He also appeared in films in the 1970s such as Bless This House, The Best Pair of Legs in the Business, Go For A Take, Carry On Behind and Carry On England. On television he will always be best remembered as factory owner Mike Baldwin in the long-running soap Coronation Street (1976-2006), but he has also appeared in hit series such as The Saint, No Hiding Place, Department S, The Persuaders, Softly, Softly and Holby City.

Johnny Briggs has semi-retired from acting although he is still active in the trade.

BROWN, Gaye

Born in Twickenham, London, in 1941, Gaye Brown appeared in one episode of On The Buses. In the Series 4 episode called 'The Canteen Girl' she had a large role as Molly, who worked in the canteen and was all set to move away with Inspector Blake and settle down on a farm in the countryside.

Her career has seen film appearances in classics such as The Clockwork Orange and The Rocky Horror Picture Show. On the small screen she had drama roles in The Borderers and Z Cars, but her speciality tended to be comedy work. She appeared in classic comedy series such as Nearest and Dearest, The Goodies, Only Fools and Horses and Last of the Summer Wine.

Gaye Brown is still acting and recently appeared in the Oscar-winning film Sweeney Todd: The Demon Barber of Fleet Street.

BRYANT, Sandra

Sandra Bryant was born in 1945 in Edgware, London. She was a regular in the seventh and last series of On The Buses, appearing as clippie Sandra in four episodes: 'Olive's Divorce', 'What the Stars Foretell', 'The Allowance' and 'Gardening Time'. She also had a large role in Holiday On The Buses, playing holiday camp employee Sandra who dates Stan.

Her acting career extended to film work, with a role in Wuthering Heights, but she was more active on television, appearing in Z Cars, Doctor Who, Special Branch, Whatever Happened to the Likely Lads?, The Fenn Street Gang and Not on Your Nellie.

BUSH, Maurice

Maurice Bush played the part of a busman nicknamed Basher in the Series 6 episode 'Private Hire', lending Stan money but threatening him with violence if he didn't pay it back on time.

His acting career saw him with roles in hit series throughout the 1960s and 1970s including Dixon of Dock Green, Doctor Who, Budgie and New Scotland Yard. His comedy roles came in Doctor in the House, Hark at Barker, The Fenn Street Gang and Love Thy Neighbour. His most notable film role came in the horror film The Creeping Flesh.

Sadly, Maurice Bush passed away in 1999.

BUX, Ishaq

Born in Kampur, India, in 1917, Ishaq Bux made one appearance in On The Buses in the Series 3 episode 'The Snake'. He played Ahmed, one of the Indian busmen at the Indian social event at the bus depot at which a snake dance is performed.

Ishaq Bux had a very active career on film and television, mainly in bit-part roles. On the big screen he appeared in Carry On Emmannuelle and Octopussy (both uncredited roles) as well as A Passage to India and Raiders of the Lost Ark. Television roles varied in genre and included Dixon of Dock Green, Department S, The Onedin Line, Softly, Softly, Crown Court, It Ain't Half Hot Mum, Minder and The Jewel in the Crown.

In 2000 Ishaq Bux passed away at the age of eighty-three.

C

CALDICOT, Richard

Richard Caldicot was born in London in 1908. In the Series 1 episode called 'Bus Driver's Stomach' he played Doctor Clark, who calls in at the Butlers to examine Stan following his complaints of stomach pains.

An acting career that ran for almost fifty years saw him appear in comedy films Follow a Star, Dentist on the Job, You Must Be Joking and Adventures of a Plumber's Mate. His television career was packed and included appearances in The Adventures of Robin Hood, Oliver Twist, Steptoe and Son, Richard the Lionheart, HMS Paradise, The Prisoner, Randall and Hopkirk (Deceased), The Beverly Hillbillies, The Avengers, Please Sir!, Catweazle, Fawlty Towers, Minder, Clarence, Casualty and Bergerac, to name but a few.

Richard Caldicot continued acting up until his death in 1995 at the age of eighty-seven.

CAMPBELL, Gavin

Born in Letchworth, Hertfordshire, in 1946, Gavin Campbell appeared in the first On The Buses film in 1971. He played the motorcycle policeman who stops Blakey from backing the bus up off the motorway and orders him to carry on down to the next intersection.

He is probably best remembered as a co-presenter of the long-running consumer programme That's Life (1982-1994), but he did make a handful of other television appearances, most notably in Softly, Softly although he also had roles in Department S, UFO, The New Avengers and Grange Hill.

Gavin Campbell now works as a media coach, lending his expertise and experience as he trains potential future TV presenters.

CARBY, Fanny

Fanny Carby was born in Sutton, South London, in 1925. The Series 5 episode of On The Buses called 'Canteen Trouble' saw her play the part of Gladys, the new canteen cook, who is brought in by Inspector Blake to stop pilfering. It is revealed that she used to be a prison warden.

She boasted an acting career that extended to almost fifty years and her dramatic television roles included appearances in Crossroads, Dixon of Dock Green, Z Cars, The Sweeney, Coronation Street, The Bill and David Copperfield. Her comedy roles were plentiful in hit sitcoms such as Till Death Us Do Part, Nearest and Dearest, The Fenn Street Gang, Love Thy Neighbour, Sykes, Birds of a Feather and Goodnight Sweetheart. She was also involved in the Spike Milligan creations Q5 and the controversial Curry and Chips. Her most notable film roles came in Sparrows Can't Sing, The White Bus and The Elephant Man.

Fanny Carby died in 2002 at the age of seventy-seven.

CARNELL, Mike

Mike Carnell played the part of the milkman in the Series 3 episode 'The Squeeze'. He calls round at the Butler house in search of payment of his bill, which sends the family ducking for cover under the table.

His film and television career has been sporadic, but he has appeared in hit series such as Only Fools and Horses, Big

Deal, Hi-De-Hi!, Tales of the Unexpected, The Bill, Jack the Ripper and You Rang, M'Lord?. Small roles also came in films Arthur Arthur and Little Dorrit.

Mike Carnell is still a regular on the pantomime and stage scene to the present day.

CARPENTER, Derek

Derek Carpenter's appearance in On The Buses came in the Series 4 episode 'Dangerous Driving'. He played the part of a young busman called Joe, who mocks Stan about his age in the canteen and is soon put in his place.

A short television career saw him appear in Crossroads, Grange Hill and Tales of the Unexpected. He has since gone into a career on stage, prop-making and also writing stage shows and plays.

CASSON, Maxine

Maxine Casson appeared in the Series 7 episode of On The Buses called 'The Football Match', adopting the role of Mary, a player in The Basildon Bashers football team that is set to take on The Luxton Lions.

During her acting career she appeared in several hit sitcoms including Doctor at Large, The Goodies, Bless This House, The Liver Birds and My Wife Next Door. Saucy film roles came in Love is a Splendid Illusion, Confessions of a Driving Instructor and Escort Girls.

Maxine Casson has now retired from acting.

CHAFFEY, Nicolette

Nicolette Chaffey played the part of the nurse seen in the bus depot in the Mutiny On The Buses film.

Her career as an actress in the UK failed to take off and her only other credited role came in the television wartime drama The Pathfinder. She turned her attention to the USA and appeared in the film The Shot and the hit television series The Practice.

Nicolette Chaffey still plies her trade as an actress, in recent years working on stage in the USA.

CLAPTON, Patricia

Patricia Clapton appeared in two episodes in Series 3 of On The Buses as a clippie called Edna. In 'Radio Control' she played a clippie undergoing training on how to operate the radio control system aboard Stan's bus, and in 'Nowhere to Go' she is homeless and moves in as a lodger with the Butlers.

Her television appearances came in series such as Z Cars, Ghost Squad, Dixon of Dock Green, The Gold Robbers, Wicked Women and The Bill. She is still active on stage in the UK.

CLARE, Elyse

Elyse Clare appeared in the Series 3 episode 'The New Uniforms', playing a clippie who picks up a magazine that Blakey has dropped, She is shocked to find it full of pictures of semi-nude women and Stan tells her it is to be the new uniform.

Her only other UK television role came in the hit sitcom Love Thy Neighbour, but she also had a small role in the Australian film Starstruck in 1982.

COCKBURN, Peter

Peter Cockburn never appeared on television in person, but his voice can be heard in the Series 5 episode of On The Buses called 'The New Telly', when commentating on a football match that Stan, Arthur and Jack are watching while visiting Blakey in his sickbed.

His voice can be heard as a narrator in a documentary shown in the cinema scene at the start of the classic comedy film Carry On Camping and also as a commentator during an episode of the crime drama Paul Temple.

CONNOR, Patrick

Patrick Connor appeared in one episode in Series 2 of On The Buses. In 'Bon Voyage' he played Nobby, who hands Stan his holiday tickets and details and warns him about excess baggage.

His lengthy acting career on television included drama roles in Quatermass and the Pit, No Hiding Place, Dixon of Dock Green, Danger Man, The Avengers, Randall and Hopkirk (Deceased), Z Cars, Poirot, The Bill and Casualty, and he made frequent sitcom appearances in series such as Doctor in the House, Please Sir!, For the Love of Ada, Dad's Army, Romany Jones and Boon.

COOK, Jacqui

Jacqui Cook's On The Buses appearance came in the Series 6 episode 'Love is What You Make It', when she played a clippie who enters the canteen just after Stan has spilt his breakfast down his uniform and she remarks what a messy eater he is.

Her acting roles were limited to the big-screen horror film Captain Kronos – Vampire Hunter and small-screen roles in Turnbull's Finest Half Hour, Are You Being Served?, Angels and The Knowledge. Her acting career saw credits dry up in 1979.

COOMBS, Pat

Pat Coombs was born in London in 1926 and played the part of new female bus driver Vera in the original On The Buses film. Vera is constantly tormented by Stan and Jack and eventually crashes her bus.

Her acting career spanned over more than forty years, appearing in classic films such as A Stitch in Time, Carry On Doctor, Carry On Again Doctor, Willy Wonka and the Chocolate Factory, Dad's Army and Ooh...You Are Awful. Her comedy roles in television saw her star in the sitcom Beggar My Neighbour and she also made appearances in Hancock's Half Hour, Up Pompeii!, Here Come the Double Deckers, Till Death Us Do Part, On The Buses spin-off Don't Drink the Water and In Sickness and in Health. She also had roles in dramas EastEnders and Doctors late in her life.

Sadly, in the mid-1990s Pat Coombs was diagnosed with severe osteoporosis, and although she bravely continued with her acting career she passed away in 2002 at the age of seventy-five.

COSTELLO, Deirdre

Deirdre Costello's On The Buses role came in the Series 4 episode called 'Not Tonight', playing the part of Molly, a clippie. Stan asks her out on a date, but she refuses as she is taking her granny to the bingo.

Her career as an actress includes a role in the hit comedy film The Full Monty and another notable big-screen appearance in The Elephant Man. Her television career saw her in a range of drama and comedy roles. She appeared in hit dramas Upstairs Downstairs, Dixon of Dock Green, Within These Walls, The Sweeney, Coronation Street, Grange Hill, Emmerdale and Doctors. Many hit sitcom roles also feature in her career including Whatever Happened to the Likely Lads?, Nearest and Dearest, Love Thy Neighbour, Mind Your Language and also I Didn't Know You Cared, which offered her a starring role.

Deirdre Costello's acting career carries on to the present day after more than forty years in the trade.

CROCKER, John

Born in London in 1925, John Crocker appeared in the Series 7 episode of On The Buses called 'The Poster'. He played the judge on the panel that has to decide which driver's face will be used on a promotional poster. On announcing Stan as the winner he remarks how proud Inspector Blake must be of him.

Throughout his long career he has worked on many classic television series, with drama roles in Emergency Ward 10, No Hiding Place, The Baron, The Avengers, The Saint, Softly, Softly, Upstairs Downstairs, Bergerac and Poirot. His comedy roles came in sitcoms such as Whatever Happened To The Likely Lads?, Waiting for God and Lovejoy.

CUNDELL, Pamela

Pamela Cundell was born in Croydon, Surrey, in 1926. Her role in the original On The Buses film saw her play Ruby, who is one of the new female bus drivers. She complains to Blakey about the dirty windscreen on her bus and later can be seen bursting into tears when the depot manager shouts at her for following false diversion signs.

Her career as an actress has included roles on the big screen such as Mrs Brown, You've Got a Lovely Daughter, Half a Sixpence and the spin-off film Love Thy Neighbour. Her television roles were largely of the comedy variety, most notably in Dad's Army but also appearances in The Benny Hill Show, The Liver Birds, Bless This House, Are You Being Served?, Only When I Laugh and In Sickness and in Health, to name but a few. Drama roles came in Dixon of Dock Green, Z Cars, Big Deal, The Borrowers, Casualty, A Touch of Frost, Doctors and EastEnders.

Her late husband was none other than Scottish actor Bill Fraser. Pamela Cundell is still active in pantomime and on stage.

CUNNINGHAM, Pauline

Pauline Cunningham appeared in two episodes of On The Buses. In her first appearance she played Brigit, a Swedish woman, in the Series 3 episode 'The New Uniforms'. Brigit and her friend mistake Stan and Jack in their new uniforms for a couple of airline pilots. In the Series 6 episode 'No Smoke Without Fire' she played a clippie called Frieda who is placed on Stan's bus as a trainee but the bus ends up breaking down.

Her acting career saw her credits restricted to television roles, with appearances in dramas such as Out of the Unknown, Z Cars, Man at the Top and The Sweeney. She also appeared in the sitcoms Two in Clover and Love Thy Neighbour, with her final credits coming in 1976 in Play for Today.

CURTIS, Alan

Born in Coulsdon, Surrey, in 1930, Alan Curtis appeared in one episode of On The Buses in Series 4. In 'The Canteen Girl' he played Inspector Stewart, who is set to replace Blakey as he is planning to move to the countryside with his girlfriend.

Roles on the big screen include small parts in Carry On

Henry, Carry On Abroad and Tomorrow at Ten. His television appearances have been wide and varied, including parts in The Saint, Crossroads, Doctor Who, The Corridor People, Z Cars, The Morecambe and Wise Show, Footballers' Wives and Last of the Summer Wine, and he has also had a busy stage career. He suffered a stroke in 1995 but has since made a return to acting.

D

DALBY, Lynn

Lynn Dalby was born in Harrogate, North Yorkshire, in 1947. Her On The Buses role came in the Series 3 episode 'Busmen's Perks'. She played the part of Janet, the depot manager's secretary, who pops into the maintenance department just as Stan is attempting to get his hands on two tins of paint.

Her most notable roles came in Crossroads, Emmerdale Farm, Budgie and Breakaway. She also appeared in the horror film Legend of the Werewolf and the sitcom Doctor in the House. It was in the 1980s, after divorcing from her husband, that she emigrated to Australia where she has continued her acting career.

DAVENPORT, Claire

Born in Sale, Cheshire, in 1933, Claire Davenport's first of three On The Buses appearances came in the original film in 1971, in which she played Peggy, one of the new female drivers, who is seen in an embarrassing position by a vicar on the upper deck of her bus. She also appeared as the canteen cook, Mrs Webb, in two Series 7 episodes of On The Buses, namely 'Friends in High Places' and 'The Allowance'.

Her acting career extended to classic films such as The Return of the Pink Panther, The Elephant Man and Return of the Jedi as well as the less successful films Carry On Emmannuelle and Adventures of a Plumber's Mate. On television her drama roles included parts in Doctor Who, Crossroads, The Baron, Z Cars and Minder. She appeared in a plethora of comedy roles such as The Rag Trade, George and the Dragon, Love Thy Neighbour, Fawlty Towers, George and Mildred, Mind Your Language and In Sickness and in Health.

Sadly, a series of strokes in the 1990s brought an untimely end to Claire Davenport's acting career and in 2002 she passed away after suffering renal failure at the age of sixty-eight.

DAVIDSON, Peter

Peter Davidson's single On The Buses appearance came in a Series 7 episode called 'The Perfect Clippie', in which he played an irate, tough passenger who is fed up with the service aboard Stan's bus.

On the big screen he had roles in Adolf Hitler – My Part in His Downfall, The Incredible Sarah and The Elephant Man, among others. He also appeared in television dramas such as The Adventures of Black Beauty, The Professionals, The Onedin Line, Secret Army, All Creatures Great and Small, The Gentle Touch and Juliet Bravo. He also took on comedy roles in The Goodies and Romany Jones.

DAWKINS, Paul

Born in 1919, Paul Dawkins' one appearance in On The Buses came in Series 7 in an episode called 'On the Omnibuses'. He played the bus depot manager in Stan's dream about what work would have been like at the beginning of the twentieth century.

His acting career offered a host of drama roles on television in series such as No Hiding Place, The Baron, The Avengers, Public Eye, Z Cars, Softly, Softly, The Onedin Line, Wuthering Heights and All Creatures Great and Small, to name but a few. He also appeared in the sitcoms Nearest and Dearest and The Worker. His most notable big-screen roles came in Far from the Madding Crowd, Universal Soldier and Dad's Army.

Paul Dawkins passed away in 1979 at the age of sixty.

DENTON, Geoffrey

Geoffrey Denton, born in 1904, appeared in one episode of On The Buses. In the Series 1 episode 'Olive Takes a Trip' he played the part of an elderly gentleman aboard Stan's bus who considerately offers to go and get an ill Olive a glass of water from a nearby café.

During his long acting career he had roles in big-screen productions including Horrors of the Black Museum, The Snake Woman and Nothing But the Night. Television drama roles were his forte, appearing in The Vise, The Secret Garden, The Saint, No Hiding Place, The Troubleshooters, Z Cars and War and Peace. Apart from On The Buses the only other notable sitcom role during his career was in And Mother Makes Three.

Geoffrey Denton passed away in 1976.

DE ROSA, Franco

Born in Viareggio, Italy, in 1944, Franco De Rosa had a fair-sized role in the Holiday On The Buses film. He played Luigi, the chef at the holiday camp, who doesn't take kindly to Stan's advances towards his sister, Maria.

His career as an actor included roles in films such as The Stud, Drop Dead Darling and That Lucky Touch as well as parts in continental productions. He also appeared in a number of hit British television series, including Paul Temple, Dixon of Dock Green, Jason King, Spy Trap, Love Thy Neighbour and Q.E.D.

DONOGHUE, Carolae

Carolae Donoghue appeared in Holiday On The Buses as holidaymaker Doreen, who goes on Stan and Jack's 'Moonlight Mystery Tour' with her friend but is forced to try to push the bus after it sinks into the wet sand on the beach.

The only other acting credit of her career came with an appearance in the hit comedy sketch show Monty Python's Flying Circus.

DOUGLAS, Sally

Born in 1942, Sally Douglas appeared in two episodes of On The Buses. In the Series 2 episode 'Bon Voyage' she played a clippie called Eileen, whom Stan asks to pose for a photograph as he demonstrates to Blakey his and Jack's ploy to attract women on their forthcoming holiday. Her second role came in Series 3 in 'Brew It Yourself' when she played a clippie that Stan makes a pass at when he is drunk following his sampling of some home brew.

Although her acting career was fairly brief, she appeared in a host of classic films such as Carry On Jack, Carry On Spying, Carry On Cleo, The Intelligence Men, Genghis Khan, Carry On Cowboy, Carry On Screaming, Carry On Follow That Camel and The Assassination Bureau. Her television roles included parts in An Arabian Night, No Hiding

Place, Danger Man, Dad's Army and Doctor in the House.

Sadly, Sally Douglas was struck down with cancer later in life and died in 2001.

DOWDESWELL, Caroline

Born in Oldham in 1945, Caroline Dowdeswell appeared in the On The Buses and Mutiny On The Buses films. In both spin-offs she played clippie Sandra, who appears as Stan's new conductress at the end of the first film. In Mutiny On The Buses she can be seen with the rest of the clippies proving to Blakey that they are wearing nothing but their uniforms.

Her acting career extended to sixteen years and was limited to television roles except for her parts in the On The Buses films. She appeared in Softly, Softly, Z Cars, Dad's Army, Casanova, Murder Must Advertise and Man About the House.

In 1978 she retired from acting and she is now involved in the publishing trade.

DUGGAN, Terry

Terry Duggan, born in London in 1932, appeared in a total of five episodes of On The Buses as well in as the original film. His first role came in the Series 1 episode 'Olive Takes a Trip', playing an angry passenger who complains about the bus service when Stan has to stop the bus as Olive falls ill. In the Series 3 episode 'The Cistern' he played the shopkeeper of the plumbing store and in the Series 4 episode 'The Anniversary' he played a passenger aboard Stan's bus with a big pet dog. The Series 5 episode 'The Inspector's Pets' saw him play a taxi driver who calls in at the Butler house and finally in the Series 6 episode 'Stan's Worst Day' he played a character called Norman, who is seen painting Stan's bus after it gets scratched. In the On The Buses film he played the part of Nobby, who works in Maintenance and supplies Stan and Jack with diversion signs.

His acting career included a role in the blockbuster film 2001: A Space Odyssey, playing the ape killed by a leopard at the start of the film. Other big-screen roles included Poor Cow, The Horror of Frankenstein and What's Up Nurse!. He also appeared in a number of classic television sitcoms, including Please Sir!, Are You Being Served?, Mind Your Language and Only Fools and Horses. Drama roles came in Randall and Hopkirk (Deceased), Manhunt, Dixon of Dock Green, Return of the Saint, The Bill and Poirot.

Husband to On The Buses star Anna Karen, Terry Duggan suffered from long-term illness in his later years and sadly passed away in 2008 aged seventy-six.

DUNBAR, Philip

Philip Dunbar appeared in two episodes of On The Buses. In Series 5 he played the barman in 'The Epidemic' and in the Series 6 episode 'Bye Bye Blakey' he played a busman who chats to Stan and Jack about the present they intend to buy Blakey, whom they believe is gravely ill.

As an actor he has had big-screen roles in recent years in the form of Amazing Grace, Mike Bassett: England Manager and The Football Factory. His television career stretches over more than forty years, with appearances in The Avengers, Paul Temple, New Scotland Yard, Z Cars, Now and Then, Never the Twain, The Bill and Devices and Desires.

DUNCAN, Juliet

Juliet Duncan's sole acting credit came in the 1972 spin-off film Mutiny On The Buses, in which she played the part of a clippie called Gladys,

DYER, Hal

Hal Dyer appeared in one episode of On The Buses and also in the Holiday On The Buses film. In the Series 5 episode 'The New Nurse' she had a large role as Mary, the new nurse at the bus depot who becomes the Butlers' lodger and catches the eye of Arthur. In Holiday On The Buses she played the camp manager's wife, Mrs Coombs, who is seen when Stan is trapped under a bed as the couple return early from a night out.

Her acting career included a role in the film The Stud, but her television credits were more numerous. She appeared in dramas such as Z Cars, The Baron, Within These Walls, Ruth Rendell Mysteries and The Bill, and her comedy roles included Doctor at Large, The Fuzz, Robin's Nest, Rentaghost and George and Mildred. She is the widow of the late On The Buses star, Michael Robbins.

E

EAST, John M.

John M. East, born in London in 1932, appeared in the very first episodes of On The Buses called 'The Early Shift', playing a busman named Lofty, who is seen welcoming Stan into the depot. His second appearance came in Series 6 in 'Stan's Worst Day', when he played the mechanic who comes to repair Stan's bus.

He had a varied career in both film and television, with his earlier days dedicated to roles on the small screen in such programmes as No Hiding Place, Doctor Who, Romany

Jones and The Fosters. Towards the end of the 1970s he moved into adult film work, including roles in The Playbirds, Confessions from the David Galaxy Affair and Emmanuelle in Soho. He also wrote scripts for and produced these films.

In 1999 he suffered a stroke and subsequently remained in ill health until his death in 2003.

EDWARDS, Percy

Born in Ipswich, Suffolk, in 1908, Percy Edwards' On The Buses contribution came in the Series 4 episode 'The Kids' Outing'. He was responsible for the bird impersonations heard when Blakey tries to entertain the restless children in the depot canteen.

His great talent as a bird impressionist and his ability to mimic other animal noises saw him supply voices for a range of films, including Santa Claus, Alien, Orca and Labyrinth. He was similarly employed on television in A Life of Bliss, The Good Life, Ripping Yarns, The Goodies, Just William and Sorry, to name but a few.

Percy Edwards passed away in 1996 at the age of eighty-eight.

ENGLISH, Shirley

Shirley English had two uncredited roles in the films On The Buses and Mutiny On The Buses. She played a member of the canteen staff in the first film and can be seen getting off the bus in the second spin-off film.

Her career as a bit-part actress saw her with uncredited roles in three 'Carry On' films: Carry On Matron, Carry On Girls and Carry On Emmannuelle. She also appeared in the television sitcoms Some Mothers Do 'Ave 'Em and Are You Being Served?.

F

FIELDER, Harry

Harry Fielder, born in 1940 in Islington, London, had an uncredited role in the Mutiny On The Buses film, in which he played the part of a floral-shirted busman involved in the darts match in the canteen.

His acting career spans over thirty years and as a bit-part actor he boasts a great array of film and television credits. On the big screen he had uncredited roles in no fewer than five 'Carry On' films as well as parts in Quatermass and the Pit, Chitty Chitty Bang Bang, Bless This House, The Likely Lads and the blockbuster sci-fi film Star Wars. Countless classic television series such as Randall and Hopkirk (Deceased), The Two Ronnies, Steptoe and Son, Softly, Softly, The Sweeney, Fawlty Towers, Z Cars, Space: 1999, Shoestring, Blake's 7, Doctor Who and Minder are just a few of the shows that he has appeared in during his packed career.

FLYNN, Kenneth

Kenneth Flynn appeared in the Series 5 On The Buses episode called 'The Kids' Outing', playing the part of one of the troublesome children. He can be seen helping to pour a bag of sugar into the petrol tank of the bus. This was his solitary role in what proved to be a brief flirtation with an acting career.

FOOT, Moira

Born in Northampton in 1953, Moira Foot appeared in the original On The Buses film, playing the part of a clippie called Katy.

Her career as an actress saw her chiefly in comedy roles in

television shows such as Hark at Barker, Doctor at Large, Are You Being Served?, The Benny Hill Show and most notably 'Allo 'Allo, but drama roles also came her way in Quiller and The New Avengers.

FRANCIS, Eric

Eric Francis, born in Manchester in 1917, appeared in two episodes of On The Buses. His first role came in Series 4's 'Nowhere to Go', playing a character called Joe, a Maintenance Department employee at the depot who fixes Blakey's hairdryer. His character appeared again later in Series 4 in an episode called 'Cover Up', in which he supplies Stan with a roll of material to re-upholster the Butlers' furniture.

His acting career embraced film roles in Make Me an Offer, Hand in Hand, Theatre of Blood, The Meaning of Life and Confessions of a Pop Performer, among others. The pick of his television roles came in Doctor Who, Z Cars, Some Mothers Do 'Ave 'Em, Dixon of Dock Green, Love Thy Neighbour, Going Straight, Chancer and The Bill.

Sadly, Eric Francis passed away in 1991 at the age of seventy-four.

FRASER, Helen

Born in Oldham, Lancashire, in 1942, Helen Fraser appeared in the Series 5 On The Buses episode 'Boxing Day Social'. She played Arthur's sister Linda who, along with her mother, comes to visit the Butlers for Christmas and Jack is seen making advances towards her.

Her acting career has offered her big-screen roles in Billy Liar, Joseph Andrews, Repulsion and Gorillas in the Mist, among others. Her television career has been extensive, with drama roles in Z Cars, Dixon of Dock Green, Coronation Street, Casualty and Tales of the Unexpected and a starring role in Bad Girls. A host of comedy roles have also filled her career, including parts in Doctor in the House, The Dustbinmen, Man About the House, Doctor in Charge, Rising Damp, The Dick Emery Show, One Foot in the Grave and The Royle Family.

Helen Fraser's acting career continues to the present day.

FULLER, Tex

Tex Fuller appeared in two of the spin-off films, On The Buses and Mutiny On The Buses, as a bus conductor called Harry. In On The Buses he can be seen sitting on the platform of the bus with a flask, but he falls off when Stan takes him by surprise and drives off in a hurry in a bid to escape Betty's husband. In Mutiny On The Buses he can be seen talking to Jack when Stan is on the upper deck of the bus with Suzy at the start of the film.

His career included roles as a bit-part actor and also a much sought-after stuntman, working as the latter in classic films such as From Russia with Love, Casino Royale (1967), You Only Live Twice, Where Eagles Dare, Superman II, A View to a Kill and Willow. Acting roles on the big screen came in Carry On Constable, Blood from the Mummy's Tomb and Nuns on the Run, and television appearances in The Avengers, Z Cars, The Two Ronnies, Citizen Smith and The Professionals also are to his credit.

FULLERTON, Shiranee

Shiranee Fullerton appeared in the Series 1 episode called 'The Canteen', playing Mrs Sharma who is brought in by Stan to take up the position of canteen cook. As it turns out she can't speak a word of English and her Indian cuisine doesn't go down well with the busmen. This was the only acting credit of her career.

G

GARROD, Keith

Keith Garrod made one appearance in the Series 4 On The Buses episode called 'The Kids' Outing'. He played one of the chief troublemakers among the children and can be seen pouring a bag of sugar into the bus's petrol tank.

His acting career never developed and this remains his sole acting credit.

GATTI, Gigi

Gigi Gatti, born in Cagliari, Italy, in 1936, was given a fair-sized role in Holiday On The Buses, playing an Italian member of staff called Maria at the holiday camp. Stan attempts to have a night of passion with her but things go wrong.

Apart from Holiday On The Buses her acting career was restricted to television roles, appearing in Public Eye, The Liver Birds, Dixon of Dock Green and Survivors.

In the 1980s she retired from acting, going on to gain qualifications in psychotherapy and work in that field. Sadly, she died of cancer in Italy in 2003 at the age of sixty-seven.

GAYNOR, Avril

Avril Gaynor's one appearance in On The Buses came in Series 2 in an episode called 'Self-Defence'. She played clippie Joyce, who demonstrates her self-defence skills on Stan during classes at the bus depot.

Her acting credits were scarce on both the big and small

screen, but she was active on stage and in pantomime. Her solitary film role came in Mini Weekend and her only other television appearance came in the BBC drama Katy.

Avril Gaynor took a break from acting to bring up her family and run a music business, but she has since resumed her career as a stage actress.

GILBERT, Kenneth

Kenneth Gilbert appeared only once in On The Buses, in a Series 7 episode called 'The Poster'. He played the chemist that Stan visits to purchase some beauty creams in an attempt to improve his appearance.

His career in acting has been very much television-oriented, largely in drama roles. Appearances in Sir Francis Drake, Crossroads, Z Cars, Callan, Special Branch, The Adventures of Black Beauty, Doctor Who, The Sweeney, House of Cards, Poirot and Midsomer Murders are the pick of his credits.

GILLIES, Carol

Born in Keighley, Yorkshire, in 1941, Carol Gillies' single On The Buses appearance came in the Series 7 episode 'The Football Match', in which she played Eunice, the captain of The Basildon Bashers team.

During an acting career that extended more than twenty years, she appeared in the films The Hiding Place, From a Far Country and Baby Boom, and her television credits included roles in I, Claudius, Within These Walls, Metal Mickey, Shoestring, Widows, Jane Eyre, The Jewel in the Crown, The Black Tower, Campion and Casualty.

At the age of just fifty, Carol Gillies passed away in 1991.

GODFREY, Tommy

Tommy Godfrey, born in Lambeth, South London, in 1916,

appeared in the Series 3 episode of On The Buses called 'Mum's Last Fling'. He played the part of the Romeo conductor Wilfred Philips, who dates Mrs Butler despite being married.

His acting career saw him with roles in a number of films such as Passport to Pimlico, Till Death Us Do Part, Bless This House, From Beyond the Grave, Love Thy Neighbour and The Great Muppet Caper. His television roles were mostly of the comedy variety in series such as Till Death Us Do Part, On the House, Steptoe and Son, Sykes, The Goodies and most notably Love Thy Neighbour and Mind Your Language. He also had his share of drama roles, appearing in The Avengers, The Saint, Nicholas Nickleby, Z Cars, Dixon of Dock Green, Doomwatch, Follyfoot and The Persuaders.

Tommy Godfrey died in 1984 at the age of sixty-eight.

GOGAN, Brenda

Brenda Gogan was given a fair-sized role in the original On The Buses film, playing an Irish canteen cook called Bridget. Stan dates Bridget but the romance dies a death when she sees a pregnant Olive just as things are heating up between them.

Her only other acting credits came in television roles in The Sinners and Budgie. She brought a halt to her acting career and is now involved in coaching actors.

GRAHAM, Laura

Laura Graham appeared in the Series 5 episode of On The Buses called 'The Nursery', playing a clippie. Her character is seen rushing to drop off her baby at the newly opened nursery in the bus depot.

Her acting work has involved mainly small-screen roles in series such as Dixon of Dock Green, Z Cars, Spy Trap, Just

William and Worzel Gummidge.

GRANT, Tiberius

Tiberius Grant was the stage name given to Bob Grant's pet cat, which appeared in the Series 7 episode called 'Gardening Time'. Called Tibbles in the actual episode, the cat is sent into Blakey's garden to create havoc and make a mess in order to scupper his chances of winning the gardening competition.

GRAY, Ian

Ian Gray made his single On The Buses appearance in the Series 4 episode 'Nowhere to Go'. He played the part of a cleaner called Charlie, who is performing his cleaning duties when his cleansing spray brings Jack and his girlfriend coughing and spluttering off of Stan's bus.

His career as a bit-part actor has seen him in a number of television appearances in series such as Dr Finlay's Casebook, Hark at Barker, Please Sir!, Doctor in the House, The Two Ronnies, The Lovers and Dixon of Dock Green. Small film roles have included parts in Just for Fun, Breaker Morant and Ishtar.

GRELLIS, Brian

Brian Grellis appeared in one episode of On The Buses in Series 5. In 'Stan's Uniform' he played the part of George, who works in the depot's clothing store. Stan visits him in a bid to get a replacement uniform and receives a dusty uniform belonging to a retired busman.

His acting career saw him land uncredited film roles in On Her Majesty's Secret Service and Battle of Britain, and his biggest roles in television came in Z Cars (1967-1978), A Tale of Two Cities and Doctor Who. He also appeared in other classic small-screen series, including Out of the Unknown, The Fenn Street Gang, Jason King, Last of the Summer Wine, The Good Life and Threads.

GRIFFITHS, Lucy

Born in Birley, Hertfordshire, in 1919, Lucy Griffiths appeared in one episode of On The Buses in Series 7. In 'On the Omnibuses' she played an old woman sitting aboard a vintage bus in an exhibition, who asks Inspector Blake what time the bus leaves, unaware that the bus is no longer in use.

Her acting credits include a large number of bit-part roles in films such as Carry On Nurse, Carry On Constable, Carry On Regardless, Carry On Doctor, Carry On Again Doctor and Carry On Behind as well as The Green Man, Murder She Said, Murder Ahoy! and One of Our Dinosaurs is Missing, among others. Her television roles, although bit-parts, make for impressive reading and include The Prisoner, Dixon of Dock Green, Doctor in the House, Please Sir!, Here Come the Double Deckers, Ace of Wands, Z Cars and All Creatures Great and Small.

Lucy Griffiths passed away in 1982 at the age of sixty-three.

GUY, Jennifer

Jennifer Guy appeared only once in On The Buses, in the Series 7 episode called 'The Football Match'. Her character, Iris, was a player in The Basildon Bashers team.

During her career as an actress she has appeared in a number of adult films such as The Love Box, Alfie Darling, Cruel Passion and Razor Blade Smile. Other big-screen roles came in Willow and Without a Clue. Her most notable television appearances in recent years have been in Cavegirl and Harry and Cosh, but she has also had a host of comedy roles throughout her career in sitcoms such as Sykes, George and Mildred, The Cuckoo Waltz, Are You Being Served?, Chance in a Million and Birds of a Feather.

H

HALL, Cheryl

Cheryl Hall, born in London in 1950, appeared in one episode of On The Buses. In 'The Epidemic' in Series 5 she played a clippie called Eileen, who is seen dating Jack.

An extensive career in acting has seen her in film roles in Villain, The Magnificent Seven Deadly Sins and No Sex Please: We're British, among others. Her biggest role in television came in the sitcom Citizen Smith, but she has also had notable parts in You and the World, Smith, Doctor Who, Bless This House, Lucky Feller, The Men's Room and The Bill. She has a host of other television credits to her name and she is still active as an actress today.

HALL, Frederick

Frederick Hall appeared in one Series 6 episode of On The Buses. In 'Stan's Worst Day' he played the depot manager who appears to rebuke Blakey during one of Stan's reminiscences in which Blakey damaged a bus when he was a driver.

His career as an actor involved a number of roles in television dramas, including No Hiding Place, A Tale of Two Cities, Public Eye, Softly, Softly, Z Cars, A Question of Guilt and Boon. He also appeared in sitcoms such as Doctor at Large, Doctor in Charge, The Fenn Street Gang and Beryl's Lot.

Sadly, Frederick Hall passed away in 1996.

HARE, Betty

Betty Hare's solitary but large On The Buses role came in the Series 2 episode 'Aunt Maud'. She played Aunt Maud, who comes to visit the Butlers for a few days and makes Stan, Arthur and Olive feel uncomfortable with her probing questions and observations.

Although her acting credits have not been as extensive as those of her sister, Doris, she did have film roles in Tread Softly, For the Love of Ada and Confessions from a Holiday Camp. Television appearances came in Nicholas Nickleby, Doctor in the House, Please Sir!, Roads to Freedom and Doctor in Charge.

HAYMAN, Damaris

Damaris Hayman, born in Kensington, London, in 1929, had a role in the Mutiny On The Buses film. She played the depot manager's wife, Mrs Jenkins, who can be seen attending the darts match in the canteen, which ends in a brawl.

During her acting career she played many bit-parts and was very active in films such as Bunny Lake is Missing, Love Thy Neighbour, Man About the House, Confessions of a Driving Instructor, The Pink Panther Strikes Again and Full Circle. Her television credits include Crossroads, Steptoe and Son, Here Come the Double Deckers, The Liver Birds, Doctor Who, The Sweeney, Keep It in the Family, Clarence and One Foot in the Grave.

HEATH, Suzanne

Suzanne Heath appeared in one Series 4 episode of On The Buses called 'Nowhere to Go', playing a clippie called Suzy. Stan is dating Suzy, but he has problems finding a place to do his courting with her.

Her career as an actress on film and television was brief. Her single big-screen role came in The Magnificent Seven Deadly Sins and she had television credits in Wicked Women, Doctor in the House, Please Sir!, The Pathfinders and The Fenn Street Gang.

HENRIX, Folker

Folker Henrix's sole acting credit came in the Series 7 episode of On The Buses called 'The Poster'. He played the part of one of the finalists in the contest that was held to choose a busman to appear on a promotional poster. Blakey describes him as a footballer and he is seen wearing a football kit. At the end of the contest he kicks Stan in the shins as he congratulates him on his win.

HERRINGTON, Doreen

Doreen Herrington appeared in two episodes of On The Buses. Her first role came in Series 1 in 'The New Inspector', when she played a clippie called Betty who is chastised by Stan for wearing a short skirt. In the Series 4 episode 'The Kids' Outing' she played a clippie called Eileen, who lends Stan her uniform for his Clara the Clippie routine.

She had a brief acting career, but her credits include roles in the films Poor Cow and Up the Junction. On television she appeared in No Hiding Place and The Wednesday Play prior to her final acting credits in On The Buses.

HOBBS, Nicholas

Nicholas Hobbs appeared in a Series 7 episode of On The Buses called 'The Poster'. He played McGregor, one of the contest finalists, whom Blakey describes as having 'muscles on muscles'. When Stan wins the contest McGregor congratulates him with a painful handshake.

His television and film career includes roles as both an actor and a stuntman. His acting credits have been bit-part roles in television series, most notably Doctor Who, Dempsey and Makepeace, Space: 1999 and The Darling Buds of May. As a stuntman he has worked on London's Burning, Boon, One Foot in the Grave and Little Britain. His stuntman work has also included a host of classic films such as Carry On Girls, The Eagle Has Landed, The Spy Who Loved Me, Superman, Octopussy, Indiana Jones and the Temple of Doom, Batman, Golden Eye and The Colour of Magic, to name but a few.

Nicholas Hobbs is still active in film and television to the present day.

HOLDEN, Ruth

Ruth Holden made one appearance in On The Buses, in a Series 4 episode called 'Safety First', playing the part of a bus passenger. When Stan breaks suddenly Blakey falls on top of her, ripping her blouse, and the incident is repeated later in the episode.

Her acting career has been very much television-oriented, her most notable roles coming in Coronation Street, Sam, The Cedar Tree, How We Used to Live and All Creatures Great and Small. She has also had roles in Doctor in the House, The Dustbinmen, Z Cars, Follyfoot, Bless Me, Father, Brookside and Medics.

HOWARD, Charlotte

Charlotte Howard appeared in a Series 4 episode of On The Buses called 'Not Tonight'. She played canteen employee Stella, who takes advantage of Stan while they are on a date.

She ensures that he spends all of his wages on her before giving him the cold shoulder.

Her acting career has comprised solely television credits in a range of comedy and drama roles, the pick of the bunch being in Nearest and Dearest, Father, Dear Father, Love Thy Neighbour, Bless This House, Robin's Nest, I, Claudius, Z Cars, Judge Dee, Crown Court, Angels and Ruth Rendell Mysteries.

HOY, Janice

Janice Hoy's solitary On The Buses appearance came in Series 5 in the Christmas episode 'Boxing Day Social'. She played an off-duty clippie called Beryl, who is chatted up by Arthur, much to Olive's displeasure.

Her only other television credit came five years earlier in 1966 in two episodes of Doctor Who.

J

JANE, Melanie

Melanie Jane appeared in two episodes of On The Buses, both in Series 7. In 'The Football Match' she played an unnamed depot canteen employee who gives Stan and Jack a cup of tea during their training for the football match. In 'Hot Water' her character was a clippie called Joyce who visits Jack's house in the hope of indulging a night of passion, but their plans are foiled by interruptions from the Butlers.

Her acting credits spanned over just a year and were limited to television roles in both drama and comedy. Drama appearances came in The Rivals of Sherlock Holmes, Dixon of Dock Green and Dial M for Murder, and her comic roles included Seven of One, The Fenn Street Gang and Oh Father.

JENNINGS, Ernest

Ernest Jennings' On The Buses appearance came in the last ever episode called 'Gardening Time'. He played the part of a rag-and-bone man and is seen with his horse and cart. Blakey and Jack see his appearance as an opportunity to get some manure for their gardens.

His career as a bit-part actor has seen him with film roles in The Reckoning, Games That Lovers Play, Futtocks End, Tales from the Crypt and Psychomania, among others. Television roles came in Dixon of Dock Green, The Goodies, Steptoe and Son, The Naked Civil Servant, Kizzy, Secret Army, Bless Me, Father and Doctor Who, to name but a few.

JOYCE, Yootha

Born in Wandsworth, London, in 1927, Yootha Joyce had a big role in the Series 7 episode of On The Buses called 'The Allowance'. She played the part of a new clippie called Jessie, who causes problems for Blakey when she demands a special payment to cover the cost of using public toilets while on duty.

She had an illustrious career in acting and is best remembered for her starring role as Mildred Roper in the hit sitcom Man About the House and its spin-off George and Mildred. Comedy roles were her speciality, but she also took on drama roles, appearing in Z Cars, No Hiding Place, The Saint, Dixon of Dock Green, The Avengers and Manhunt. Her comedy credits include parts in Steptoe and Son, George and the Dragon, The Fenn Street Gang and Seven of One. Her career on the big screen saw her with credits in Sparrows

Can't Sing, Fanatic, A Man for all Seasons, Nearest and Dearest, Man About the House and George and Mildred.

Tragically, after years of battling with alcoholism, Yootha Joyce died of liver failure in 1980 at the age of fifty-three, with screen husband and good friend Brian Murphy at her bedside.

K

KERR, Fraser

Fraser Kerr, born in Glasgow in 1931, appeared in two episodes of On The Buses. In the very first episode 'The Early Shift' he played the part of the television interviewer who appears at the picket line during the bus strike and interviews Stan. In Series 3 in 'Radio Control' he is seen briefly as the airline pilot receiving a message from Stan, who is on the wrong airwave.

As an actor his film credits include Carry On Regardless and Theatre of Death. He took on a variety of roles in television series such as Dixon of Dock Green, Dr Finlay's Casebook, Doctor in the House, Mind Your Language, Kidnapped and Howards' Way. He was perhaps most occupied with radio projects and he worked on a number of drama broadcasts.

Fraser Kerr fell victim to cancer and died in 2000 at the age of sixty-nine.

KESSLER, Catherine

Catherine Kessler made her single On The Buses appearance in the Series 6 episode 'Bye Bye Blakey'. She played the part of the nurse who summons Stan to see the depot's doctor.

Her film and television credits span over twelve years and include big-screen roles in Groupie Girl and Murder By Decree. Her most notable appearance on television was her role in The Fenn Street Gang, but she also had roles in Softly, Softly, Z Cars, Dixon of Dock Green, George and Mildred and Within These Walls, among others.

KETTLEWELL, Ruth

Born in Worcester in 1913, Ruth Kettlewell became a familiar face in On The Buses, appearing in three episodes. Her first appearance came in Series 3 in 'First Aid', playing a nurse aboard Stan's bus who asks for his help in delivering a passenger's baby. Next was a Series 5 role in 'The Nursery' playing the strict and grumpy nurse in charge of the depot's new nursery. Finally, in Series 5 again, in 'The Epidemic' she played the depot nurse who gives the staff their inoculations.

Although not a household name during her acting career, she appeared regularly on our screens, with film credits in Friends and Neighbours, Sons and Lovers, Zeppelin and The Black Panther. A wide range of small roles in television included parts in The Onedin Line, Juliet Bravo, The Dick Emery Show, All Creatures Great and Small, Inspector Morse and Heartbeat as well as roles in children's series such as Catweazle, Worzel Gummidge and Here Come the Double Deckers.

Ruth Kettlewell passed away in London in 2007 at the age of ninety-four.

L

LAND, Mary

Mary Land appeared in a Series 6 episode of On The Buses called 'No Smoke Without Fire'. She played clippie Suzy on whom Jack practises the kiss of life during a fire drill.

Her film and television career consists of a handful of credits spread over seven years. On the big screen she appeared in the adult films Her Private Hell and Loving Feeling prior to taking on television roles. Her credits on the small screen include Armchair Theatre and Within These Walls.

LAWRENCE, Andrea

Andrea Lawrence's first acting encounter with On The Buses came in the first spin-off film. She played the memorable character known in the film as 'Turnaround Betty' and Jack is seen visiting her during his shifts for bouts of passion. Her second role came in Series 5 in 'Canteen Trouble' as canteen employee Suzy, who is giving Stan and Jack extra helpings of food.

Her acting career saw her with a number of film credits, including Countess Dracula, For the Love of Ada, Love Thy Neighbour, Frankenstein And The Monster From Hell and Man About the House. On television she was to appear primarily in comedy roles in series such as It's A Square World, Doctor At Large, The Fenn Street Gang, The Goodies and Doctor In Charge. Her drama roles came in No Hiding Place, Softly Softly, Van der Valk and Dixon Of Dock Green.

LIND, Gillian

Born in India in 1904, Gillian Lind's sole On The Buses appearance came in the Series 5 episode 'Boxing Day Social'.

She played the part of Arthur's mother, who comes to stay with the Butlers over the festive period.

Her film roles spanned from the early 1930s through to the early 1970s and included The Man Outside, Dick Turpin, Open All Night, Aunt Clara, Don't Talk to Strange Men and Fear in the Night. Her television career began in the early years of its introduction, with roles in Clive of India, On the Spot and Nine Till Six. In later years her most notable roles came in Pride and Prejudice, Nicholas Nickleby and Emma and she also had parts in dramas such as Dixon of Dock Green, Man in a Suitcase, The Saint and Upstairs Downstairs.

Gillian Lind died in 1983 at the age of seventy-nine.

LINEHAN, Barry

Barry Linehan was born in Ireland in 1925 and had a fair-sized role in the Mutiny On The Buses film. He played the part of the policeman in his patrol car who is mistakenly contacted by Inspector Blake and ordered to return to the depot at once. He reports to the depot and promptly confiscates the radio control system and berates the Inspector.

His acting career stretched over more than thirty years in both film and television. His big-screen credits include Witchcraft, The Devil-Ship Pirates, Suburban Wives and Bullseye. His most notable television roles came in Whiplash, The Andromeda Breakthrough, The Protectors, Big Breadwinner Hog, Ace of Wands, Z Cars and The Tomorrow People. His comedy parts included appearances in The Likely Lads, Curry and Chips, Some Mothers Do 'Ave 'Em, Love Thy Neighbour and Dad's Army, among others.

Barry Linehan passed away in 1996 at the age of seventy.

LITTLEWOOD, Frank

Frank Littlewood made one appearance in On The Buses in the Series 3 episode 'Mum's Last Fling'. He played the commissionaire at the gas board headquarters who points Stan in the direction of the lift.

In an acting career that extended to a quarter of a century he had big-screen credits in Meet the Duke and Dangerous Voyage. His television credits were varied and included Hancock's Half Hour, No Hiding Place, Steptoe and Son, The Man in the Iron Mask, The Onedin Line and Please Sir!.

LODGE, David

David Lodge, born in Strood, Kent, in 1921, had roles in the first two spin-off films. In On The Buses he played the part of a busman who can be seen complaining to Stan when Olive is having difficulties in the canteen and also is seen later complaining to Jack about Stan fraternising with a female bus driver. His character in Mutiny On The Buses was the safari park guard who briefs Stan and Blakey on the park's protocol before they enter.

His career as an actor may not have offered an abundance of starring roles, but he appeared regularly on both the small and big screen. His film credits came in classic war films such as The Silent Enemy, The Safecracker, No Time to Die, Ice Cold in Alex, Yesterday's Enemy, The Long Ships and Guns at Betasi, among others. He was also a familiar face in classic comedy films such as Up the Creek, Watch Your Stern, The League of Gentlemen and A Shot in the Dark as well as a range of Norman Wisdom films. He also featured in five 'Carry On' films: Carry On Regardless, Carry On Girls, Carry On Dick, Carry On Behind and Carry On England.

Despite all of his activity on the big screen he was equally as busy in television roles, both drama and comedy. His most notable drama appearances came in Ghost Squad, The Saint, Gideon's Way, Randall and Hopkirk (Deceased), The Avengers, The Champions, Z Cars and Dixon of Dock Green. He was a common figure in comedy roles, most notably in Tottering Towers and Lovely Couple but he also featured in Love Thy Neighbour, The Reg Varney Revue, The Fenn Street Gang, Carry On Laughing and It Ain't Half Hot Mum.

Later in life David Lodge was struck down by cancer and he died in 2003 at the age of eighty-two.

LOVEGROVE, Arthur

Born in Fulham, London, in 1913, Arthur Lovegrove made one On The Buses appearance in the Series 1 episode 'Bus Driver's Stomach'. He played Harry, a bus driver who fails his medical but gets transferred to a job as Inspector.

His acting career saw him appear in a number of films from the late 1940s up until the early 1980s. His big-screen credits included Passport to Pimlico, Meet Simon Cherry, Genevieve, The Runaway Bus, Safari, The Two Faces of Dr Jekyll, Crooks Anonymous, Carry On Cowboy and Eye of the Needle. His television credits were varied and included The Avengers, No Hiding Place, Dixon of Dock Green, Z Cars, Catweazle, Please Sir!, Bless This House and Shoestring. In addition to acting, he was also an accomplished playwright.

He continued working as an actor until his death in 1981 at the age of sixty-eight.

LYNN, Tara

Tara Lynn appeared in the Holiday On The Buses film. She played the part of a holidaymaker, Joyce, who goes on Stan and Jack's 'Moonlight Mystery Tour' but ends up having to walk home when the bus becomes beached.

Her short acting career was limited to small roles in adult films such as Secrets of a Door-to-Door Salesman, Commuter Husbands and Take an Easy Ride.

She now works in the make-up departments in the film industry.

LYONS, John

John Lyons, born in London in 1943, appeared in four episodes of On The Buses. His debut came in Series 4 in 'The 'L' Bus', playing the part of Bert, a trainee bus driver, who while training aboard Stan's bus is forced to help use the bus as a removal van. In the following episode, 'The Kids' Outing', he played the same role and can be seen asking Inspector Blake who will be the driver for the children's outing. His third appearance came in the Series 7 episode 'Goodbye Stan', in which he played the part of a busman called Bill, who is seen in the depot mocking Blakey as he arrives with all of his belongings and is seen later in the pub having a farewell drink with Stan. His final appearance came in 'The Allowance', playing the character Sid, a busman who is seen at the start of the episode having a cup of tea with Jack in the canteen and is later seen driving the bus.

His career as an actor encompassed film, television and stage roles. His big-screen credits include Dr Jekyll and Sister Hyde, Yellow Dog, Sweeney 2 and Blues Brothers 2000. His most notable television role was playing the character DS Toolan in A Touch of Frost (1992-2008) and his other drama roles include Z Cars, UFO, Upstairs Downstairs, The Sweeney, The Bill, Doctors and Spooks. Parts in comedy have also been plentiful, most notably in The Nineteenth Hole but also in The Liver Birds, Doctor in Charge, Romany Jones,

Man About the House, Yus My Dear, Spooner's Patch, Mind Your Language and George and Mildred, to name but a few.

John Lyons' acting career has continued apace to the present day.

M

MADDEN, Peter

Born in Malaysia in 1904, Peter Madden had a small part in the original On The Buses film. He played the part of Mr Brooks, who judges Stan's performance on the skidpan test after he has an accident and awards him with pass marks.

His career as a bit-part actor spanned over forty years in both film and television. On the big screen his credits included The Wicked Lady, Fiend Without a Face, Battle of the V-1, Exodus, From Russia with Love, Doctor Zhivago and One of Our Dinosaurs is Missing. His television roles included Danger Man, No Hiding Place, King of the River, The Troubleshooters, Z Cars, Sherlock Holmes, The Saint, The Avengers, Steptoe and Son and Hadleigh.

Sadly, Peter Madden passed away in 1976 at the age of seventy-one.

MAHONEY, Janet

Janet Mahoney had a large role in the 1972 film Mutiny On The Buses. She played the part of Stan's fiancée Suzy, who eventually calls off the wedding rather than move in with the Butlers.

Her acting credits ranged over seven years and saw her appear on the big screen in Carry On Loving and Doctor in Trouble. Television comedy roles came her way in Howerd's Hour, Up Pompeii! and Dad's Army.

MAKUNDA, Vemu

Vemu Makunda appeared in one episode of On The Buses in Series 3. In 'The Snake' he was the musician who plays the backing music as Fatima performs her snake dance and can be seen playing the stringed instrument.

This role was his only acting credit as he was a musician first and foremost.

MARSHALL, Alex

Alex Marshall's sole On The Buses appearance came in the Series 5 episode 'A Thin Time'. She played a clippie called Beryl who catches Arthur's eye, leading him to invest in a wig in a bid to impress her.

As an actress her screen credits were all on the small screen and were almost exclusively drama roles in such series as Z Cars, Crossroads, Dixon of Dock Green, Germinal, Coronation Street, Budgie and New Scotland Yard, among others.

MARTYN, Larry

Born in London in 1934, Larry Martyn appeared in two Series 7 episodes of On The Buses. He played the part of Fred, who replaces Stan as Jack's driver, in 'What the Stars Foretell' and 'Gardening Time'.

His acting career consisted mainly of bit-part roles in both film and television. His big-screen credits include The Great St Trinian's Train Robbery, Carry On at Your Convenience, For the Love of Ada, Carry On Behind and Omen III: The Final Conflict. On the small screen he appeared in No Hiding Place, Dixon of Dock Green, Z Cars, Up Pompeii!, For the Love of Ada, Love Thy Neighbour, Dad's Army, Whoops Baghdad and most notably Spring and Autumn and

Are You Being Served?.

Larry Martyn died in 1994 at the age of sixty.

MAXTED, Mary

Mary Maxted had a small role in Series 6 of On The Buses in an episode called 'Private Hire'. She is seen briefly playing the mother of a clippie called Iris. This role was her only comedy credit.

Her acting career saw her gain other credits in small-screen dramas such as Tales of the Unexpected, The Pickwick Papers, London's Burning and The Bill.

McGARRY, Parnell

Parnell McGarry appeared only once in On The Buses, in a small role in the Series 3 episode called 'The Inspector's Niece'. She played a trainee clippie who gives Jack a far from memorable shift.

Her career as an actress saw her with a few credits in film and television between 1967 and 1973. On the big screen she appeared in adult films such as Big Zapper and The Love Ban as well as the comedy films Bedazzled, Up the Chastity Belt and Up the Front. On television her most notable roles came in the sitcoms The Fenn Street Gang and Dad's Army.

McGEE, Henry

Born in Kensington, London, in 1929, Henry McGee was given a fair-sized role in the final spin-off film Holiday On The Buses in 1973. He played the part of Mr Coombs, the manager of the holiday camp.

His acting credits spanned over half a century and he will be best remembered as the straight man to Benny Hill for a number of years. He had small film roles in Sailor Beware,

The Italian Job, Revenge of the Pink Panther and Carry On Emmannuelle. His most notable comedy roles in television came in The Benny Hill Show (1971-1988), The Worker and Let There Be Love, but he also appeared in comedy classics such as The Goodies, Doctor in Charge, Rising Damp, Sykes and It Ain't Half Hot Mum. Although rare, drama roles did come his way, for instance in No Hiding Place, Take a Pair of Private Eyes, The Saint and The Avengers.

Sadly, Henry McGee was struck down by Alzheimer's disease late in life and died in 2006 at the age of seventy-six.

McGRATH, Maggie

Maggie McGrath's sole On The Buses role came in the first spin-off film, in which she played the part of Gladys, one of the newly recruited female bus drivers.

In her long acting career she had big-screen credits in English Without Tears, The Body Said No, Intent to Kill, The Great St Trinian's Train Robbery, All the Way Up and The Jigsaw Man, to name but a few. Television roles were less frequent during her career, but credits included Armchair Theatre, Thriller, Hammer House of Mystery and Suspense and From the Top.

McKILLOP, Don

Don McKillop, born in Carlisle in 1929, appeared in a Series 5 episode of On The Buses called 'The Inspector's Pets'. He played the role of Harry, a busman who sees the damage to Stan's bus and tells him that if Blakey goes on holiday and he takes over as temporary Inspector he will turn a blind eye to all the damage.

His acting career largely revolved around television, with his only notable roles on the big screen coming in Otley and

An American Werewolf in London. On the small screen he had drama roles in Gideon's Way, King of the River, Dr Finlay's Casebook, Doctor Who, Sutherland's Law, Z Cars, The Professionals and C.A.T.S. Eyes as well as comedy parts in The Likely Lads, The Liver Birds and Rosie.

Don McKillop died in 2005 at the age of seventy-six.

McNAB, Bob

Born in Huddersfield in 1943, Bob McNab appeared in the Series 7 episode of On The Buses called 'The Football Match'. He played Bob, a busman whose talents are so good that Jack feels he will win the match for The Luxton Lions on his own. He can be seen demonstrating his skills when juggling a football in the training session at the depot.

His role in On The Buses was his only venture into acting, as he was in fact a professional footballer and went on to have an illustrious career with Arsenal.

MENDEZ, Julie

Julie Mendez (credited as Julia Mendez in On The Buses) appeared in one Series 3 episode called 'The Snake'. She played the part of canteen employee Fatima, who performs a snake dance in the depot canteen at a social event.

She had other acting credits in roles involving dancing, as she was a professional dancer by trade. Her big-screen credits included The Night We Dropped a Clanger, Panic, She and Theatre of Death. She can also be seen performing a dance in the opening titles sequence of the James Bond film From Russia with Love, and on television she appeared as a dancer in Virgin of the Secret Service. She also worked on a handful of films as a dance choreographer, one of which was Carry On Up the Khyber.

MERCER, Olive

Olive Mercer made one appearance in On The Buses, in the Series 4 episode called 'Cover Up'. She played the part of an elderly passenger who reports a missing earring to Inspector Blake and he has to search Stan's bus.

Her acting career revolved largely around television roles. Comedy parts came most notably in Dad's Army, but she also featured in Please Sir!, Doctor in Charge, The Perils of Pendragon and Whatever Happened to the Likely Lads?. She also had credits in dramas such as Crossroads, Within These Walls, Angels and Dixon of Dock Green. Her solitary big-screen role came in Sex and the Other Woman.

MICHAELS, Anna

Anna Michaels appeared in the 1971 spin-off film On The Buses. She played clippie Eileen, who is seen at the start of the film.

This was to be the only acting credit of her career.

MILLER, Sandra

Sandra Miller appeared in two episodes of On The Buses, both in Series 5. In 'The Best Man' she played the part of Sally, a clippie and also Inspector Blake's niece, who is preparing to get married. She played the same character in 'The New Nurse' and is seen asking why the Inspector is standing with his trousers hitched up after he has an accident aboard Stan's bus.

Her career as an actress, although a lengthy one, offered only a handful of film and television credits. Her big-screen credits were in the adult films Titillation and Girls of Hollywood Hills, and on television she appeared in Victoria Regina, Bergerac and Pictures.

MILLS, Madeleine

Madeleine Mills appeared in three episodes of On The Buses. Her first role came in Series 3 in 'The Inspector's Niece', playing a clippie called Sally. Stan and Jack both take a fancy to her and compete for her affections. In another Series 3 episode called 'Going Steady' she played the same character, who is in a serious relationship with Stan and marriage seems to be on the cards for the couple. Her final appearance was as a clippie called Christine in the Series 5 episode 'Vacancy for Inspector'. She works aboard Stan's bus, but her endless appetite is very off-putting.

Her credits as an actress were confined entirely to television roles in drama and comedy. Drama appearances came most notably in Doctor Who and Softly, Softly but also included Swizzlewick, The Rivals of Sherlock Holmes and Z Cars. She had comedy roles in Please Sir! and its spin-off The Fenn Street Gang.

MITCHELL, Norman

Born in Sheffield, Yorkshire, in 1919, Norman Mitchell appeared in two episodes of On The Buses and also in one of the spin-off films. His first role came in the Series 3 episode 'Busmen's Perks'. His character was Nobby, who works in the Maintenance Department and supplies Stan with paint and paintbrushes from the storeroom at the depot. His next appearance came in the film On The Buses, in which he played the part of the London Transport official at the skid-pan, who shows Inspector Blake one of their buses. His final appearance saw him reprise his role of Nobby in the Series 5 episode 'Stan's Uniform'. We see Stan and Jack seek his help in a bid to remove paint from Stan's new uniform.

His acting career spanned fifty years and he was regarded

as one of the hardest-working actors in the business, as his endless list of credits in film and television bear witness. His big-screen credits included Carry On Cabby, Carry On Spying, Carry On Cleo, Carry On Screaming, The Great St Trinian's Train Robbery, Half a Sixpence, Nearest and Dearest, Man About the House, Legend of the Werewolf, The Pink Panther Strikes Again and Carry On Emmannuelle, among others. A vast array of television roles came his way, with his most notable appearances coming in Lorna Doone, The Boy with Two Heads, Z Cars, Beryl's Lot (1973-1977), George and Mildred and Worzel Gummidge. His other television roles were varied and included classic series such as The Adventures of Robin Hood, Maigret, The Saint, Crossroads, Doctor Who, The Prisoner, Whatever Happened to the Likely Lads?, Dad's Army and Are You Being Served?.

Norman Mitchell continued acting up until his death in 2001 at the age of eighty-two.

MOHAN, Ursula

Ursula Mohan was a regular supporting cast member, appearing in a total of six episodes of On The Buses. Her debut came in the Series 2 episode 'Self-Defence', in which she played a clippie called Liz. She and her friend Joyce are the objects of Stan and Jack's affections. In Series 3, she took the role of clippie Joyce in the episode called 'Radio Control'. Joyce is one of two conductresses put aboard Stan's bus in order to learn how to use the newly installed radio system. Her third appearance was in the Series 4 episode 'Nowhere to Go', playing clippie Edna who is dating Jack. Later in the Series 4 episode 'Christmas Duty' she reprises her role as Joyce and is seen coming out of the depot toilets to be met by

Jack, who kisses her under some mistletoe, and she continues her romance with Jack in a subsequent Series 4 episode called 'Not Tonight'. Her final appearance in On The Buses was in the Series 6 episode 'Private Hire', playing a secretary called Iris who needs help moving house.

Her career as an actress has encompassed a number of different television roles. In drama she has appeared in Cribb, Agatha Christie's Partners in Crime, The Bill, Ruth Rendell Mysteries, London's Burning, Kavanagh QC, Casualty and Holby City. Her comedy roles came in Agony, Pig in the Middle and 2point4 Children. She also had big-screen credits in Tell Me Lies and The Bank Job.

Ursula Mohan's acting career is still ongoing today.

MOORE, Kevin

Kevin Moore made one appearance in the very first episode of On The Buses called 'The Early Shift'. He played the part of a TV newsman, who turns up at the picket line with a television crew to report on the bus strike.

His career as a bit-part actor has seen him with credits in both film and television. On the big screen he has appeared in Ascendancy, Under Suspicion, Fierce Creatures, Fogbound and Johnny English, among others. His television roles have included parts in Z Cars, Not on Your Nellie, The Gentle Touch, A Fine Romance, Father Ted, Silent Witness, The Bill, Poirot, Heartbeat and Doctors.

MORGAN, Garfield

Born in Birmingham in 1931, Garfield Morgan made one appearance in On The Buses. In the Series 6 episode called 'Bye Bye Blakey' he played the role of Mr Stilton, the depot manager, who is seen ordering Inspector Blake to undergo a compulsory medical.

In an acting career that is fast approaching fifty years in duration, he will be best remembered for his role as DCI Frank Haskins in the classic hard-hitting police drama The Sweeney. He has appeared in several other such roles in Z Cars, Softly, Softly, Dixon of Dock Green, Minder and The Bill as well as filling a host of other drama roles. Comedy parts on television have included Two in Clover, The Train Now Standing, Keep It in the Family, The Gaffer, Hallelujah, The Nineteenth Hole, No Job for a Lady and Alas Smith and Jones. Film credits have included A Prize of Arms, Our Mother's House, Digby, the Biggest Dog in the World, George and Mildred and 28 Weeks Later.

Garfield Morgan's acting career has continued to the present day.

MORRELL, Juel

Juel Morrell (also known as Julie Morrell) appeared in two episodes of On The Buses. In the Series 4 episode called 'Safety First' she played the part of a clippie who arrives in Blakey's badly damaged office and asks why the Inspector has his head stuck between the bars on the door. In the same series in the episode called 'The 'L' Bus' she played Betty, a clippie who is being trained by Stan and Jack and is seen complaining to Blakey that her jacket is too tight.

She had only one other acting credit during her career, which came in the mid-1960s television drama United.

MORRIS, Aubrey

Aubrey Morris, born in Hampshire in 1926, made one On The Buses appearance, in the Series 6 episode called 'Love Is What You Make It'. He played the stressed marriage guidance counsellor that Stan, Olive and their mum go to for advice.

In an acting career that has run for fifty years he has many credits to his name in both film and television. On the big screen he appeared in The Quare Fellow, The Sandwich Man, The Great St Trinian's Train Robbery, Up the Junction, A Clockwork Orange and Man About the House, to name just a few. On television his drama roles have included Oliver Twist, Z Cars, The Saint, The Avengers, Man in a Suitcase, The Champions, The Sweeney, Murder She Wrote, Babylon 5 and Columbo. He has also been a familiar face in comedy roles, appearing in The Rag Trade, The Liver Birds, The Fenn Street Gang, Not on Your Nellie, Chance in a Million and Hot Metal, among others.

Aubrey Morris's acting career is still ongoing.

MOSES, Albert

Born in Sri Lanka in 1937, Albert Moses appeared in one Series 7 episode of On The Buses. In 'Friends in High Places' he played an Indian busman briefly seen in the depot canteen grimacing after eating some canteen food.

His acting career began in India before his arrival in the UK and he has largely been involved in bit-part roles. Appearances on the big screen include What's Up Nurse!, Stand Up Virgin Soldiers, The Spy Who Loved Me, Carry On Emmannuelle, An American Werewolf in London, Octopussy and East is East. His television credits include Budgie, Warship, Robin's Nest, Angels, The Chinese Detective, Juliet Bravo, The Jewel in the Crown, Tenko, Holby City and The Bill. He is best remembered for his role in the hit sitcom Mind Your Language, in which he played a Pakistani student called Ranjeet Singh.

Albert Moses is still active as an actor to this day.

MULLARD, Arthur

Arthur Mullard, born in Islington, London, in 1910, had a fair-sized role in the final spin-off film Holiday On The Buses. He played holidaymaker Wally Briggs, a somewhat common and uncharismatic character, and Olive ends up getting into his bed by mistake.

His early acting career is peppered with a whole host of uncredited roles in classic British films such as Oliver Twist, The Lavender Hill Mob, The Colditz Story, The Ladykillers and The Day They Robbed the Bank of England. His credited film roles came in Crooks Anonymous, Sparrows Can't Sing, The Great St Trinian's Train Robbery, Chitty Chitty Bang Bang, Crooks and Coronets and Adventures of a Plumber's Mate. His roles on television revolved largely around comedy, most notably in the series Romany Jones and Yus My Dear, but he also appeared in Sykes and A..., Frankie Howerd, The Benny Hill Show and Margie and Me.

Arthur Mullard died in 1995 at the age of eighty-five.

MULLINS, Bartlett

Bartlett Mullins, born in Crosby, Lancashire, in 1904, appeared in one Series 5 episode of On The Buses. In 'Lost Property' he played the part of a cleaner called Joe, who is seen finding the eaten portion of fish and chips aboard Stan's bus.

During a lengthy career as an actor he had a host of bit-part roles to his credit. On the big screen he appeared in The Wild Heart, Eight O'Clock Walk, Conflict of Wings, Half a Sixpence and Frankenstein Created Woman, to name but a few. The pick of his numerous television roles include

Clementina, Nicholas Nickleby, No Hiding Place, The Old Curiosity Shop, The Likely Lads, Dixon of Dock Green, Doctor Who, Hark at Barker, Steptoe and Son, Z Cars and Worzel Gummidge.

Bartlett Mullins died in 1992 at the age of eighty-seven.

MUNRO, Alex

Born in Shettleston in Scotland in 1911, Alex Munro had a small part in the Holiday On The Buses film. He played the part of a patient in the waiting room and is seen telling Blakey that the nurse is busy with another patient.

His acting credits were rare, but he was more renowned as a comedian and theatre performances were his speciality. The only other credits to his name came on television in Z Cars and Mr Rose in the 1960s.

He passed away in 1986 at the age of seventy-four.

N

NEWBOLD, Valerie

Valerie Newbold appeared in three episodes of On The Buses. Her debut came in the Series 1 episode 'The New Inspector' when she played a clippie called Jenny, who can be seen sitting on a bench in the depot commenting on a fellow clippie's length of skirt. Her second appearance came in the final episode of Series 1 called 'The Darts Match'. She played the same character, who is a friend of Iris, and they challenge Stan and Jack to a darts match. Finally, in the Series 3 episode 'Radio Control', she played Miss Woodhall, who is seen handing Blakey the radio system and busman's code list.

Her career as an actress failed to bring a great deal of credits. Apart from On The Buses her only other credits came on television in the late 1960s in Dr Finlay's Casebook and Nicholas Nickleby.

NIGHTINGALE, Michael

Born in Brighton, Sussex, in 1922, Michael Nightingale was offered a bit-part role in the Mutiny On The Buses film. He appeared as the pilot contacted in error by Blakey over the radio control system.

A long career in acting saw him in a number of bit-part roles in both film and television. He was a familiar face in the classic 'Carry On' series of films, appearing in Carry On Regardless, Carry On Cabby, Carry On Jack, Carry On Cleo, Carry On Cowboy, Carry On Don't Lose Your Head, Carry On Follow That Camel, Carry On Camping, Carry On Matron, Carry On Girls, Carry On Dick, Carry On England and Carry On Emmannuelle. Other film roles came in Ice Cold in Alex, Watch Your Stern, Raising the Wind, Bless This House and The Return of the Pink Panther. His career in television saw him with varying roles, most notably in Dixon of Dock Green but also in Danger Man, The Prisoner, Nearest and Dearest, Carry On Laughing and Cadfael, to name but a few.

Michael Nightingale died in 1999 at the age of seventy- six.

NORRISH, Keith

Keith Norrish became something of a regular supporting cast member in On The Buses, appearing in four episodes. His debut came in the Series 5 episode 'The Epidemic', when he played a busman called Brian who is seen sitting on a bench in the depot and sharing some chocolate with his girlfriend, Sandra. Also in Series 5, in the episode called 'The New Nurse', he played busman George and is seen telling

Jack that Blakey is visiting the nurse. His third appearance came in Series 5 again in 'The Strain' as the character George, who can be seen helping Jack to lift Stan into the driver's cab. Finally, in the following episode called 'The New Telly' he played a busman who is seen coming to collect his Christmas Club money from the Inspector.

His career as an actor involved bit-part roles exclusively on television. His credits came in a drama called Spyder's Web, Doctor Who and Blake's 7. His only other comedy role was in the classic sitcom Porridge.

NYE, Pat

Born in London in 1908, Pat Nye made one appearance in On The Buses, in a Series 7 episode called 'The Visit'. She played Inspector Blake's mother, who comes to visit her son and ruffles plenty of feathers in the Butler household.

As an actress she was seen mainly in television roles, although she did have big-screen credits in Mr Perrin & Mr Traill, Appointment with Venus and The Mirror Crack'd. Her most notable role in television came in the romantic drama Little Women, but she also appeared in No Hiding Place, Please Sir!, Z Cars, Ace of Wands, The Fenn Street Gang and Yus My Dear.

Pat Nye passed away in 1994 at the age of eighty-six.

O

OULTON, Brian

Brian Oulton, born in Liverpool in 1908, appeared in the first spin-off film, On The Buses. He played the depot manager, who can be seen throughout the film chastising Inspector Blake.

He had a very active career as an actor, with credits stretching over fifty years. The pick of his film appearances included The Million Pound Note, Doctor in the House, The Silent Enemy, Carry On Nurse, The 39 Steps, I'm Alright Jack, Carry On Constable, The Bulldog Breed, Carry On Cleo, Carry On Camping, Ooh... You Are Awful and Gandhi. Roles on television saw his most notable appearances come in Mr Digby, Darling, Doctor at Large, Scoop and The Old Curiosity Shop. He also had roles in classic sitcoms such as Hancock's Half Hour, Steptoe and Son, George and the Dragon and The Young Ones. He was also very busy in a number of stage productions.

Brian Oulton died in 1992 at the age of eighty-four.

P

PAGE, Katherine

Born in Glasgow in 1908, Katherine Page made one On The Buses appearance, in the Series 3 episode called 'Foggy Night'. She played the part of a passenger stranded aboard Stan's bus in thick fog and is seen asking Inspector Blake if everything is alright when the bus comes to a sudden halt.

She was an actress for almost seventy years before she finally retired and her television and film credits began in the early 1950s. On the big screen she appeared in Women of Twilight, The Intimate Stranger and Room at the Top, among others. Her television roles range from the dramas of The Vise, Dixon of Dock Green, No Hiding Place, Dr Finlay's Casebook, Bleak House and All Creatures Great and Small to comic roles in Sorry, Don't Wait Up, Only Fools and Horses, One Foot in the Grave and Dinnerladies.

PARKINSON, Robin

Robin Parkinson, born in Coventry, Warwickshire, in 1925, appeared only once in On The Buses. In the Series 5 episode 'The Best Man' he played the vicar, who is impatiently waiting for Stan and the bridegroom.

His career as an actor has spanned more than forty years and includes credits in both film and television. On the big screen he appeared in Billy Liar, The Family Way, To Catch a Spy, George and Mildred and The Asylum. His most notable roles on television came in The Many Wives of Patrick and 'Allo 'Allo. A whole range of appearances in classic sitcoms include roles in Whatever Happened to the Likely Lads?, The Liver Birds, Dad's Army, Love Thy Neighbour, Rising Damp, Bless This House, Terry and June and It 'Ain't Half Hot Mum. Drama roles were not uncommon either and his credits include Crossroads, Softly, Softly, The Tomorrow People, Z Cars, Van der Valk, The Professionals, The Pickwick Papers and The Bill.

PEISLEY, Frederick

Born in Finchley, London, in 1904, Frederick Peisley appeared in one Series 7 episode of On The Buses. In 'The Perfect Clippie' he played the role of the depot's doctor, who is seen giving Olive her medical.

In an acting career that began with film credits in the early 1930s, he made many big-screen appearances, including parts in The Scotland Yard Mystery, The Secret of the Loch, Gentleman's Agreement, Murder at the Cabaret, Hide and Seek and Subterfuge. He also had notable television roles in Our House and The First Churchills as well as a host of other smaller roles in such series as Dixon of Dock Green, No Hiding Place, Detective, The Avengers, Z Cars, Here Come the Double Deckers, Doctor in Charge, Emmerdale Farm, Doctor at Sea and Sykes, among others.

Frederick Peisley died in 1975 at the age of seventy.

PETERS, Arnold

Arnold Peters appeared in one Series 1 episode of On The Buses. In 'The New Inspector' he played the depot manager, who can be seen ordering Inspector Blake to remove Stan from his new post as he comforts a clippie.

His career as an actor has comprised television credits only. His most notable roles came in Germinal, Please Sir!, The Tomorrow People and London Belongs to Me, but he also appeared in dramas such as Z Cars, Softly, Softly, Hadleigh, The Troubleshooters, Dixon of Dock Green, Special Branch, The Onedin Line, The Duchess of Duke Street and Doctors as well as a variety of comedy series. The latter includes some of the best British sitcoms of all-time, such as Porridge, Dad's Army, The Fall and Rise of Reginald Perrin, It Ain't Half Hot Mum and Only Fools and Horses. His other claim to fame is that he supplies the voice of a character in the long-running radio series The Archers.

PETERS, Luan

Born in Bethnal Green, London, in 1946, Luan Peters appeared in one Series 5 episode of On The Buses. In 'Canteen Trouble' she played the part of Joan, who is in charge of the newly installed vending machine in the canteen and she can be seen giving Stan a complimentary pie.

Her acting career has encompassed a number of horror and adult films as well as credits in memorable television series. Her big-screen appearances include Man of Violence, Not Tonight, Darling, Freelance, Lust for a Vampire, Twins of Evil, The Devil's Men and Pacific Banana. She also had television credits in Coronation Street, Z Cars, Doctor Who, Robin's Nest, The Professionals, Fawlty Towers and The Bill. During the 1960s she pursued a career as a pop singer but failed to gain real recognition in that trade.

PETERS, Reginald

Reginald Peters appeared in the first spin-off film in a bit-part role. He played a medical orderly who rushes out of the hospital to meet Stan's bus when it comes to a halt outside and is promptly told to get a hammer and chisel as Olive is stuck in the sidecar.

His career in acting offered bit-part roles in films and on television. A film role in Inadmissable Evidence and television credits that included Crossroads, Paul Temple, A Room in Town, Softly, Softly and Jason King were the highlights of his career.

POWELL, Nosher

Nosher Powell, born in Camberwell, London, in 1928, made a total of four appearances in On The Buses, three in episodes and one in the first spin-off film. His debut role came in the Series 1 episode 'Bus Driver's Stomach', playing a busman called Bert, who attempts to solve Stan's stomach pains with a spot of physiotherapy in the canteen. Later in the series in the episode called 'The Canteen' he reprises the role of Bert and can be seen complaining about the food in the canteen. He also had a role in the first spin-off film, playing Betty's suspicious husband, who almost catches her in bed with Stan. His final appearance came in the Series 5 episode 'The Strain', playing a busman called Vic, who can be seen lifting up Stan's girlfriend Doreen in an attempt to guess her weight.

In a career both as a bit-part actor and as a stuntman he has had an incredible array of credits. As an actor he appeared in films that included Oliver Twist, Demetrius and the Gladiators, A Shot in the Dark, Circus of Fear, Crossplot, Nearest and Dearest, The Mackintosh Man, Carry On Dick, Krull and Willow. He also had television roles in Dixon of Dock Green, The Baron, The Saint, The Avengers, Randall and Hopkirk (Deceased), The Benny Hill Show, Monty Python's Flying Circus, The Sweeney and The Comic Strip Presents..., among others. As a stuntman he worked on the majority of the James Bond films plus a host of all-time classic epics. He was also a champion boxer prior to launching his acting career and was a sparring partner of legendary boxers such as Muhammad Ali, Joe Louis and Sugar Ray Robinson.

R

REGAN, Linda

Born in London in 1959, Linda Regan had two uncredited roles in On The Buses. Firstly, in the Series 4 episode 'Christmas Duty' she played a clippie called Edna, who gets kissed under the mistletoe by Stan at the depot. Her second appearance came in the On The Buses film made in 1971, in which she played the part of a pretty passenger aboard Stan's bus who is ogled by Jack.

Her career as an actress has seen her mainly in bit-part roles in both film and television. On the big screen she appeared in Keep It Up Jack, The Hiding Place, Confessions of a Pop Performer, Carry On England and Adventures of a

Private Eye, among others. She will be best remembered for her character April in the hit 1980s sitcom Hi-De-Hi!, but she has also had roles in Carry On Again Christmas, Special Branch, Seven Faces of Woman, Minder, The Gentle Touch, Bergerac, Over the Rainbow, The Bill, Doctors and Holby City.

Still involved in acting today, Linda Regan is also a writer of crime novels.

RENNISON, Jan

Born in Australia in 1947, Jan Rennison had a role in the Mutiny On The Buses film. She played the part of Gloria, who can be seen kissing Stan in the final scene of the film.

In her acting career she had television credits in The Persuaders and Space: 1999 and she was also a co-host on the game show Quick on the Draw. Prior to acting, she was awarded the title of Miss Australia and appeared in the 1965 Miss World beauty contest.

RHODES, Adam

Adam Rhodes had a fair-sized role in his sole appearance in On The Buses. He played Little Arthur, the troublesome son of Arthur and Olive, in the film Holiday On The Buses.

His only other credit as an actor came in the television series The Boy with Two Heads. He went on to pursue a career away from acting and now lives in Canada.

RICHARD, Wendy

Born in Middlesbrough, Cleveland, in 1943, Wendy Richard made two appearances in On The Buses. In the film On The Buses she played a housewife whose laundry ends up in the hands of Blakey, which sees him getting both a beating and acute embarrassment. In the Series 5 episode 'The Busmen's Ball' she played a clippie called Elsie, who enters the Inspector's office and finds a picture of a naked woman on his desk.

An illustrious acting career saw her with many credits in both film and television. No doubt she will be best recognised as Pauline Fowler in EastEnders (1985-2006) and Miss Brahms in the hit sitcom Are You Being Served? (1972-1985), but her other television credits include Danger Man, The Likely Lads, No Hiding Place, Up Pompeii!, Carry On Again Christmas, Please Sir!, Dad's Army and Spooner's Patch. She also appeared in a number of films, including parts in Doctor in Clover, Bless This House, Carry On Matron, Carry On Girls and Are You Being Served?. Another feather in her cap was a No. 1 hit single called 'Come Outside' in 1962, in collaboration with Mike Sarne.

Sadly, after a long fight against cancer, Wendy Richard died on 26th February 2009 at the age of sixty-five.

RICHARDSON, David

David Richardson appeared in one Series 5 episode of On The Buses called 'The New Telly'. He played the part of busman George, who brings Stan a box of goods he has bought for Christmas from the canteen.

His credits as an actor include film roles in Around the World in Eighty Days and Lust for a Vampire. On television he appeared in Mystery and Imagination, Nicholas Nickleby, Z Cars, Follyfoot and The Fenn Street Gang, among others.

RODERICK, George

George Roderick had a small role in the first spin-off film On The Buses, playing the part of a policeman. When a bus collides with a lorry he can be seen asking Inspector Blake if he is in charge of the bus.

Mainly seen in bit-part roles, quite a few of them as a policeman, he had plenty of big and small-screen credits. His film appearances included The Quatermass Experiment, The Ladykillers, A Night to Remember, Follow a Star, Carry On Again Doctor and Love Thy Neighbour. On television his most notable role came in a comedy called Three Live Wires, but he also appeared in The Vise, The Saint, The Avengers, Swallows and Amazons, Z Cars, The Champions, The Benny Hill Show and Love Thy Neighbour, among others.

Sadly, George Roderick died in 1976 at the age of sixty-two.

ROEG, Nicolette

Nicolette Roeg made one appearance in On The Buses, in the Series 6 episode called 'Bye Bye Blakey'. She played the part of the doctor who examines the staff for their medicals.

Her career as an actress spanned over thirty years, with the early part of her career seeing her appear in films of the musical variety such as My Ain Folk, Home Sweet Home, Under New Management and I'll Turn to You. Her television roles, mainly in dramas, included Here and Now, No Hiding Place, Dixon of Dock Green, Paul Temple, The Onedin Line, Z Cars and Blake's 7.

ROWLANDS, David

David Rowlands appeared in the first two spin-off films of On The Buses. In the first film he played the shocked parson on the upper deck of the bus that sees more than he bargained for when a female bus driver relieves herself. In Mutiny On The Buses he played a policeman on his beat who is contacted by mistake by Inspector Blake.

His acting career has encompassed a range of mainly bit-part roles in both film and television. On the big screen he appeared in Bless This House, Assassin, Vampira and 11 Harrowhouse. His drama roles in television came in The Regiment, Doctor Who, Rumpole of the Bailey, The Life of Henry the Fifth and The Cleopatras. He also had roles in a whole range of classic sitcoms, including Bless This House, Are You Being Served?, Love Thy Neighbour, Rising Damp, The Fall and Rise of Reginald Perrin, Terry and June and 'Allo 'Allo.

RUSSELL, Sheridan Earl

Sheridan Earl Russell appeared in the Series 4 episode of On The Buses called 'The Kids' Outing'. He played Blakey's nephew, Harold, who is among the children attending the children's outing.

His credits as an actor saw him in a handful of film and television roles. On the big screen he appeared in Bugsy Malone, Jabberwocky and The Lords of Discipline, and his television credits include I, Claudius, Scum and The Bill.

S

SALTER, Ivor

Born in Taunton in 1921, Ivor Salter made two appearances in On The Buses. In the first spin-off film he played the role of the policeman in the scene where Blakey is withholding a housewife's laundry bag, believing the contents to be Stan's. In the final episode of On The Buses called 'Gardening Time' he once again played a policeman, this time catching Blakey as he attempts to climb up a drainpipe at the back of the Butler house after being locked out.

He had a hectic acting career on film and television, mostly playing bit-part roles. His film credits included The Heart Within, Dog Eat Dog, Be My Guest, Tiffany Jones and House of Mortal Sin. His most notable television roles came in Crossroads, in which he played the deeply religious Reg Cotterill, and in Doctor Who. Other hit series in which he was involved include The Avengers, Dixon of Dock Green, Dr Finlay's Casebook, Danger Man, Z Cars, No Hiding Place, Here Come the Double Deckers, Nearest and Dearest, The Sweeney, All Creatures Great and Small and In Loving Memory.

Ivor Salter died in 1991 at the age of seventy.

SHAKESBY, Patricia

Born in Cottingham, East Yorkshire, in 1942, Patricia Shakesby appeared in one episode of On The Buses. In the Series 4 episode called 'The Injury' she played the part of the nurse in the depot seen treating Inspector Blake after he has an accident.

Her acting credits in film and television stretch back to the late 1950s. On the big screen she had roles in Offbeat, She Knows, Y'Know and He Who Rides a Tiger. She will be best remembered for her television role as Polly Urquhart in the hit BBC drama Howards' Way (1985-1989). She also appeared in Hancock's Half Hour, Coronation Street, Z Cars, The Likely Lads, The Borderers, Doctor in the House, The Liver Birds, War and Peace, Yes Minister and Sapphire and Steel, among others. She now spends her time writing plays.

SHAMSI, Mohammad

Born in Muradabad, India, in 1930, Mohammad Shamsi appeared in the Series 1 episode of On The Buses called 'The

Canteen'. He played the part of busman Mr Sharma, who suggests that Stan should give his wife the job of canteen cook.

His acting career credits include film roles in The Horsemen, The Adventures of Barry McKenzie, The Man Who Would Be King and The Hound of the Baskervilles. On the small screen he has appeared in series such as Danger Man, Special Branch, Z Cars, It Ain't Half Hot Mum and Are You Being Served?.

SHEARD, Michael

Born in Aberdeen, Scotland, in 1938, Michael Sheard appeared in six Series 7 episodes of On The Buses and also in the final spin-off film Holiday On The Buses. In all of his appearances he played the depot manager, who is seen giving Inspector Blake a hard time on several occasions. His debut came in the Series 7 episode 'The Ticket Machine' and his final appearance came in the film role.

An acting career that ran for over forty years saw him amass many credits in both film and television. His big-screen credits included parts in The McKenzie Break, England Made Me, The Hiding Place, Force 10 From Navarone, Escape to Athena, Star Wars V: The Empire Strikes Back and Indiana Jones and the Last Crusade. He will be best remembered for his television role in the children's school drama Grange Hill, in which he played the tough teacher Mr Bronson, a character who struck fear into schoolchildren everywhere at the time. He also had notable roles in Dixon of Dock Green, Softly, Softly, Auf Wiedersehen, Pet and Doctor Who. A range of other small-screen roles across the genres were plentiful, and he also won acclaim for his numerous portrayals of Adolf Hitler on film and television.

Sadly, Michael Sheard died in 2005 at the age of sixty-seven.

SINGER, Campbell

Born in London in 1909, Campbell Singer made an appearance in Series 4 of On The Buses. In ' The Lodger' he played the traffic manager Mr Nichols, who becomes a lodger at the Butler house and promptly makes a pass at Olive.

He gained many credits in both film and television in an acting career that spanned almost thirty years. In his earlier years his film roles included Operation Diamond, Hangman's Wharf, Cage of Gold, Appointment in London, Lady in the Fog, The Titfield Thunderbolt, Conflict of Wings, The Square Peg, The Fast Lady and On the Beat. From the early 1960s onwards, however, television roles predominated, with appearances in Benny Hill, Doctor Who, Take a Pair of Private Eyes, The Forsyte Saga, The Saint, The Avengers, Please Sir!, Z Cars, Dad's Army, Rising Damp and Some Mothers Do 'Ave 'Em.

Campbell Singer passed away in 1976 at the age of sixty-seven.

SINIAWSKI, Petra

Petra Siniawski appeared in one Series 6 episode of On The Buses. In 'Bye Bye Blakey' she played a clippie who turns up for her expected medical while Stan, Jack and Blakey are waiting to be examined and is told by the Inspector to leave.

Her career as an actress saw her gain uncredited roles in a handful of films in which she was able to show off her dancing skills. Appearances came in Woman in Love, The Music Lovers, Fiddler on the Roof, The Old Curiosity Shop and Billy Elliott, among others. She swapped her acting roles on film and television for stage work and became a highly regarded choreographer and director of classic stage musical productions.

SLATER, Michael

Michael Slater was a regular supporting cast member of On The Buses and appeared in a total of five episodes. His debut came in the very first episode, 'The Early Shift', in which he played the part of one of a group of television crew (seen wearing headphones), who turns up at the depot to report on the bus strike. In the Series 1 episode 'Olive Takes a Trip' he played a passenger that gets on the bus with his family and is seen asking an unwell Olive for tickets. He next appeared in the Series 4 episode 'The 'L' Bus', playing the mechanic that attempts to repair Stan's bus. His fourth role came in another Series 4 episode called 'Safety First', this time playing Joe from the Maintenance Department. He is seen bringing tools in to help free the Inspector, who is trapped between iron bars. He resumed the character of Joe in his final appearance, in the Series 4 episode called 'The Injury'. He is seen telling Stan that the step has been rigged to collapse, which is part of Stan's cunning plan to gain sick pay and compensation by having an accident at work.

His acting career was limited to television, mainly in bit-part roles, and credits on the small screen include Z Cars, The Champions, Love Thy Neighbour, Dixon of Dock Green, Romany Jones, Yus My Dear, Mind Your Language and The Bill.

SOBLOSKY, Perry

Perry Soblosky made one appearance in On The Buses, in the Series 7 episode called 'The Poster'. He played Perkins, one of the finalists in the competition to be the face on a promotional poster. His character is described as a part-time male model and he is seen berating Stan in a camp manner.

He had a brief spell of acting credits that saw him with television roles in The Adventurer and Moonbase 3. His only big-screen appearance came in the Hammer horror film Captain Kronos – Vampire Hunter.

STEEDMAN, Shirley

Shirley Steedman appeared in a Series 5 episode of On The Buses called 'The New Telly'. She played a naive clippie called Eileen, who collects her Christmas Club money and then tells Stan and Jack that Blakey got her in the club, much to their amusement.

Her credits as an actress spanned over twelve years and included a role in the film The Prime of Miss Jean Brodie. On the small screen she appeared in Dr Finlay's Casebook, Whatever Happened to the Likely Lads?, Edward the Seventh, Open All Hours and Penmarric.

STENSGAARD, Yutte

Born in Thisted, Denmark, in 1946, Yutte Stensgaard had one role in On The Buses. In the Series 3 episode called 'The New Uniforms' she played a Swedish woman called Ingrid. She and her friend Brigit are attracted to Stan and Jack when they are wearing their new uniforms, as they mistake them for airline pilots.

Her brief career as an actress may only have seen credits spread over five years, but they were hectic times. She appeared in a number of horror films, such as Scream and Scream Again, Lust for a Vampire and Burke and Hare as well as adult films, including Zeta One, A Promise of Bed and an uncredited role in Carry On Again Doctor. On the small screen she was a hostess on the hit game show The Golden Shot as well as having roles in The Saint, Doctor in the House, Jason King and The Persuaders, among others.

She emigrated to the United States in 1972 and for many years worked in radio broadcasting.

STEWART, Reginald

Reginald Stewart's sole appearance in On The Buses came in the Series 4 episode 'The 'L' Bus'. He played a trainee driver called Alf, who is seen briefly throughout the episode and at one point is told by Inspector Blake to get out of the driver's cab.

His career as an actor consisted of a series of bit-part roles on television, including The Fenn Street Gang, Law and Order, Secret Army, The Gentle Touch, The Adventures of Sherlock Holmes, The Bill and Miss Marple.

SUTCLIFFE, Clare

Clare Sutcliffe's only role in On The Buses came in the Series 4 episode 'Dangerous Driving', in which she played the part of clippie Pat. Stan takes a shine to Pat and attempts a new dance called 'The Shake' with her in the depot canteen.

Her acting credits include film roles in I Start Counting, The Best Pair of Legs in the Business and The Ploughman's Lunch. On television she appeared in Softly, Softly, Manhunt, Z Cars, Coronation Street and Thriller as well playing other roles in less notable television series.

SWEENEY, Maureen

Maureen Sweeney appeared in the film Holiday On The Buses, playing holidaymaker Mavis. Stan tries to date her but is continually thwarted by her bossy mother.

In an acting career spanning over forty years her credits have been largely television-based, although big-screen roles did arise in The Squeeze and Sorted. Her most notable television role came in the sitcom Romany Jones, but she also appeared in Crossroads, The Sweeney, Within These Walls, That's My Boy, Dempsey and Makepeace, Only Fools and Horses, Running Scared, The Bill and Casualty.

T

TODD, Bob

Born in Faversham, Kent, in 1921, Bob Todd made two appearances in On The Buses. He had a role in the Mutiny On The Buses film as the new Inspector, who takes over at the depot after Blakey is demoted to conductor. He is seen displaying the same mannerisms as his predecessor and stepping in to take a new clippie for a cup of tea just as Stan is chatting her up. His second role came in the Series 7 episode 'Friends in High Places'. He played Mr Simpson, who briefly takes charge at the depot and turns out to be an old friend of Mrs Butler.

In his career as a comedy actor he will be best remembered for his role as a straight man to comedy legend Benny Hill, appearing in a number of series spread over twenty years. He did find time for many other comedic roles in such series as It's a Square World, Around with Allen, Please Sir!, Carry On Again Christmas, Inn for a Penny (his only starring role), The Fenn Street Gang, Doctor at Sea and Funny Man, to name but a few. He also appeared in a number of films, including Postman's Knock, Hot Millions, Carry On Again Doctor, Scars of Dracula, That's Your Funeral, Digby, the

Biggest Dog in the World, The Four Musketeers and Superman III.

Sadly, Bob Todd passed away in 1991 at the age of seventy.

V

VARNEY, Jeanne

Jeanne Varney, the daughter of the late, great Reg Varney, appeared in the first spin-off film On The Buses. She played a character called Mavis, whose friend's laundry ends up in the hands of Blakey. She is seen hitting the Inspector with her handbag and accuses him of being a 'knicker-snatcher'.

This was the only acting credit in her career.

VASEY, Suzanne

Suzanne Vasey appeared in the Series 3 episode of On The Buses called 'First Aid'. She played a clippie called Rose, who administers first aid to Blakey after he injures his leg in an accident aboard Stan's bus.

Her acting credits were confined to television roles in The Man in Room 17, Mrs Thursday, Softly, Softly, Department S and Wicked Women. Her television appearances ended there, but she had roles on stage in the 1970s.

W

WALKER, Rudolph

Born in Trinidad and Tobago in 1939, Rudolph Walker appeared in the very first episode of On The Buses, 'The Early Shift'. He played a busman called George, who is seen on picket duty with Stan and Jack during the bus strike.

During an acting career that has spanned forty years, he has thrived in comedy and drama roles on television and in film. He gained notoriety for his role as West Indian Bill Reynolds in the hit 1970s sitcom Love Thy Neighbour and two decades later he had a major role in the comedy The Thin Blue Line. Since 2001 he has also cemented a role in the popular soap opera EastEnders, and his other television appearances have included The Champions, Doctor Who, Hadleigh, New Scotland Yard, The Chinese Detective, Boon, Rules of Engagement, The Bill, A Perfect State and Doctors. He has also had roles in films such as The Witches, Universal Soldier, 10 Rillington Place, Love Thy Neighbour, Spaghetti House, King Ralph and Hit for Six. His acting career still continues apace today.

WALKER, Sue

Sue Walker made an appearance in the Series 2 episode of On The Buses called 'Late Again'. She played clippie Ada, who is disturbed when Stan climbs through a window into the depot's ladies toilet and calls him a peeping Tom.

Her only other credit as an actress came in the television sitcom Oh, Father!

WALLER. Kenneth

Born in Huddersfield, Yorkshire, in 1927, Kenneth Waller made one appearance in Series 5 of On The Buses. In 'Boxing Day Social' he played a busman seen wearing a paper Christmas hat and announcing that everyone should take their partners as its time for another dance.

His career as an actor saw him appear in both classic television series and films. On the big screen he had roles in Room at the Top, Chitty Chitty Bang Bang, Scrooge, Fiddler on the

Roof and Carry On Behind. His best-known role on television was as the grandfather in the classic sitcom Bread, but he also had notable roles in Big Deal and Are You Being Served?. Other small-screen credits included Crossroads, The Fenn Street Gang, Dixon of Dock Green, Z Cars, The Professionals, Doctor Who and All Creatures Great and Small.

Kenneth Waller died in 2000 at the age of seventy-two.

WALTER, Jules

Jules Walter made two appearances in On The Buses, his first role coming in the Series 7 episode 'The Football Match'. He played a busman called Chalkie, who is chosen to be in the football team and is seen during the training session at the depot. He played the same character later in the same series in an episode called 'Goodbye Stan', in which he is seen standing at the bar next to Jack as they have one last drink with Stan.

His acting credits, in both film and television, all came in the 1970s. He appeared in the films Can You Keep It Up for a Week? and The Wild Geese and in the television series The Onedin Line, Some Mothers Do 'Ave 'Em, The Professionals and Blake's 7.

WALTERS, Hugh

Born in Mexborough, Yorkshire, in 1939, Hugh Walters made one appearance in On The Buses. In the Series 5 episode 'The Best Man' he played the part of Bill, the busman who is to marry the Inspector's niece, Sally. He is seen going out with Stan and Jack on his stag night and getting drunk.

Over forty years of acting credits in film and television have seen him chiefly on the small screen, with big roles in Nicholas Nickleby and Chance in a Million. He also appeared in many classic television series, such as Doctor at Large, The Fenn Street Gang, Jason King, The New Avengers, Z Cars, Shine On Harvey Moon, Doctor Who, Casualty, The Russ Abbot Show, Cor Blimey!, Heartbeat and Doctors. His film credits include Catch Us If You Can, Rocket to the Moon, Alfie Darling and Firelight.

WARD, Dervis

Born in Dowlais, Wales, in 1923, Dervis Ward made a brief appearance in the Mutiny On The Buses film. He played an angry passenger, who is seen asking Jack when he can get on the bus at the very start of the film and again in a similar scene towards the end of the film.

His career as an actor saw him appear in a number of big-screen roles, including parts in The Chiltern Hundreds, Murder Anonymous, The Long Haul, Ben Hur, The World of Suzie Wong, The Loneliness of the Long Distance Runner, The Violent Enemy, To Sir, with Love, Dad's Army and Crossed Swords. On television his credits came in The Adventures of Robin Hood, Dial 999, Z Cars, Gideon's Way, Dixon of Dock Green, The Avengers, The Champions, Here Come the Double Deckers and The Protectors.

Dervis Ward died in 1996 at the age of seventy-two.

WARWICK, Gina

Gina Warwick made one appearance in On The Buses, in the Series 4 episode 'Safety First'. She played a nurse, who can be seen telling Stan that she has just given Inspector Blake a blanket bath.

Her acting career saw her gain a handful of credits from

the mid-1960s until the early 1970s. Film roles came in A Man for All Seasons, Mister Ten Per Cent, Carry On Follow That Camel and The Haunted House of Horror. On television she appeared in We Have Ways of Making You Laugh, Department S and Play for Today.

WATTS, Gwendolyn

Born in Carhampton, Somerset, in 1937, Gwendolyn Watts made two appearances in On The Buses, both in Series 1. Her first appearance came in the episode 'The New Conductor' as a clippie called Iris, who is put on Stan's bus and they get on very well. She reprised the role in 'The Darts Match', in which she and her friend get involved in a contest and a bet with Stan and Jack.

Her career as a comedy actress saw her appear in many hit television series and classic films. On the big screen she had roles in Billy Liar, Sons and Lovers, My Fair Lady, Fanatic, The Wrong Box, Carry On Doctor, Carry On Again Doctor and Carry On Matron. Comedy roles on television were commonplace and she appeared in classics such as The Rag Trade, Steptoe and Son, The Benny Hill Show and Love Thy Neighbour as well as playing a starring role in Sorry I'm Single. Drama roles also came her way in Alfred Hitchcock Presents, The Avengers, Maigret, Z Cars and Coronation Street, among others.

Gwendolyn Watts died in 2000 at the age of sixty-two.

WATTS, Queenie

Born in London in 1926, Queenie Watts had a fair sized-role in the Holiday On The Buses film. She played the part of a holidaymaker called Lily Briggs, who is seen berating her husband, Wally, firstly when believes that he has found a toilet among the bushes and again when Olive mistakenly gets into bed with him.

As a comedy actress she appeared in a host of classic sitcoms. She will be best remembered for her starring roles in Romany Jones and its spin-off Yus My Dear alongside Arthur Mullard, in which she portrayed the same character that she had played in Holiday On The Buses. Her other most notable television roles came in sitcoms such as Up Pompeii!, Dad's Army, The Goodies, Steptoe and Son, Sykes, Beryl's Lot and George and Mildred. On the big screen she appeared in Sparrows Can't Sing, Alfie, Half a Sixpence, Poor Cow, Up the Junction, All Coppers Are .... and Schizo.

Sadly, she was to be diagnosed with cancer and died in 1980 at the age of fifty three.

WELLS, Elaine

Elaine Wells appeared once in On The Buses, as a chemist's assistant in the Series 7 episode 'The Poster'. She is left to serve Stan when he is looking to buy a range of beauty products.

An acting career that spanned almost twenty years saw her credits confined solely to television roles. She appeared in dramas such as Crossroads, Dr Finlay's Casebook, Coronation Street, Within These Walls and Edward and Mrs Simpson. Her only comedy role came in On The Buses.

WEST, Nina

Nina West made one Series 7 appearance in On The Buses. In 'What the Stars Foretell' she played a clippie called Wendy, who is seen reading horoscopes in a magazine with her friend, Sandra, at the start of the episode.

In a brief run of credits she made one big-screen appearance in the sex comedy Adventures of a Plumber's Mate. Her television roles came in The Rivals of Sherlock Holmes and The Fenn Street Gang.

WESTHORPE, Wayne

Wayne Westhorpe made an appearance in the 1972 spin-off film Mutiny On The Buses. He played Little Arthur (the son of Olive and Arthur), who is seen throughout the film causing mischief.

This was his only acting credit and in later life pursued a different trade.

WHITTER, Glen

Glen Whitter has the distinction of being the most used supporting cast member in On The Buses. He played a West Indian clippie nicknamed Chalkie and made credited appearances in nine episodes of On The Buses from 1970 to 1972 as well as featuring in a number of other episodes in an uncredited capacity. His debut appearance came in the Series 3 episode 'Brew It Yourself' and his final part came in the Series 6 episode 'Union Trouble'.

His acting career never really took off, but he did have a small part in the cult 1980 film Flash Gordon. His only other credits came in television in The Troubleshooters and Doctor in the House and he also had an uncredited role in an episode of Doctor Who.

WILD, Jeanette

Jeanette Wild made two appearances in On The Buses, one on the big screen and the other in a Series 7 episode. She appeared in the first spin-off film as a clippie called Suzy, who is seen telling Stan that he must be joking when he asks her out on a date. Her second role came in 'The Football Match', playing a member of The Basildon Bashers side called Rita, who reveals to Stan and Jack that she is a forward.

Her acting credits include big-screen roles in Her Private Hell, Zeta One, Dr Jekyll and Sister Hyde and The Fiend. She also had parts in many hit television shows of all genres, including Up Pompeii!, Z Cars, Monty Python's Flying Circus, Softly, Softly and Coronation Street. At the end of the 1970s her acting credits came to an end.

WILLIAMS, Kate

Born in London in 1941, Kate Williams made three appearances in On The Buses. In the Series 2 episode 'Late Again' she played a clippie called Doreen, who is dating Stan but their romance is hindered by his early shifts. Her second role came in Series 4 in 'The Other Woman', in which she played a clippie called Wendy who is accused of having a relationship with Arthur. Her final appearance came in the film Holiday On The Buses, when she played the nurse at the holiday camp who is dating Blakey until Jack comes along.

An acting career that has run for over forty years has seen her with credits in both film and television. Her most notable roles came in the controversial hit sitcom Love Thy Neighbour, in which she played Joan Booth (1972-1976), and in the drama Widows (1983). Her comedy roles on the small screen include credits in Please Sir!, Doctor at Large, Born and Bred, Bottle Boys, Just Good Friends, Only Fools and Horses, Alas Smith and Jones, Time After Time and May to December. She also has many drama roles to her credit, the pick of which were in Dixon of Dock Green, The Gentle Touch, Minder, C.A.T.S. Eyes, Lovejoy, The Bill, Berkeley

Square, Family Affairs and EastEnders. Her film credits include Poor Cow, Till Death Us Do Part, Love Thy Neighbour, What's Up Nurse!, Quadrophenia and Little Dorrit. Her career as an actress has continued to the present day.

Y

YOUNG, Sharon

Sharon Young appeared in the Series 5 episode of On The Buses called 'The Epidemic' as a clippie named Sandra. Stan is attracted to her and, even though she has a boyfriend, he manages to date her before he catches the flu that has swept through the depot.

Her only other acting credit was gained in her television role in The Troubleshooters and she also had an uncredited part in a 1965 episode of Doctor Who. Her role in On The Buses was to be the biggest of her career.

SUMMARY

Saturday 28th February 2009 marked the 40th anniversary of the first ever episode of On The Buses being screened on British television. Even though a generation has passed since On The Buses first graced our screens, the classic sitcom is still loved by millions of people around the world. DVD sales remain high, forums and websites dedicated to On The Buses are popular with visitors from across the globe, special On The Buses events attract much interest, and repeats of the series and the spin-off films continue to introduce a new generation of fans to this comedy phenomenon.

The great success of On The Buses can be attributed to the fantastic scripts of Ronald Wolfe and Ronald Chesney and the wonderful acting talents of the actors and actresses that made up the cast. Sadly, the majority of the On The Buses legends are no longer with us, but I would like to take the opportunity to dedicate this book to them. To Cicely Courtneidge, Michael Robbins, Doris Hare, Bob Grant and Reg Varney I say thank you for the memories and all of the wonderful laughs that your work continues to spark among the many thousands of fans, new and old, even though you are no longer with us.

REVIEWS FROM FORMER CAST MEMBERS:

"The book is an amazing reference to everyone connected with this tremendous 70's series Full of personal and happy memories for me, and a necessary addition for fans and TV historians alike."

- Hal Dyer

"A great book to dip into while you are waiting at a bus stop. It's timeless, just like 'On The Buses'!"

- Linda Regan

"Here is a well researched book full of information to please all fans. It is a must for all fans."

- Albert Moses

Lightning Source UK Ltd.
Milton Keynes UK
UKOW06f2326110716

278154UK00016B/699/P